The saucy Vegetarian

Quick & Healthful
No-Cook
Sauces & Dressings

Joanne Stepaniak

Book Publishing Company
Summertown, Tennessee

Cover design: Randa Abbas

Cover and interior photos: Digital Imagery® copyright 1999 PhotoDisk, Inc.

Interior design: Warren Jefferson, Michael Cook, Gwynelle Dismukes

Printed in the United States by

Book Publishing Company

P.O. Box 99

Summertown, TN 38483

1-888-260-8458

www.bookpubco.com

ISBN 1-57067-091-9

07 06 05 04 03 02 01 00   9 8 7 6 5 4 3 2 1

Stepaniak, Joanne
     The saucy vegetarian : quick & healthful no-cook sauces & dressings / by Joanne Stepaniak.
        p. cm.
     ISBN 1-57067-091-9 (alk. paper)
     1. Sauces. 2. Vegetarian cookery. 3. Quick and easy cookery. I. Title.
     TX819.A1.S84 1999
     641.8'14--dc21   99-058360

Calculations for the nutritional analyses in this book are based on the average number of servings listed with the recipes and the average amount of an ingredient if a range is called for. Calculations are rounded up to the nearest gram. If two options for an ingredient are listed, the first one is used. Not included are optional ingredients or serving suggestions.

Contents

Vinaigrette Sauces & Dressings
43

Nut & Seed Based Sauces & Dressings
65

Tomato, Bean & Vegetable Based Sauces and Dressings
89

Creamy Tofu Sauces & Dressings
105

Introduction

In recent times, the verb "cook" has taken on connotations typically associated with more objectionable four letter words. Well, it's high time to turn that notion around! No longer does mealtime need to be a dreaded, time-consuming, under-appreciated event. By making quick vegetarian no-cook sauces and dressings part of your everyday menus, you can enhance the flavor, attractiveness, healthfulness, and excitement of even the most banal dish.

The purpose of this book is to present a rich repertoire of recipes and ideas to stimulate the novice cook as well as the experienced gourmet. At the same time, it sheds new light on the basic concept of vegetarian cuisine and introduces a fresh approach to meal planning that dispels boredom and unleashes creativity while keeping time and effort at bay.

One of the most sensible ways to plan vegetarian meals is to give starches and whole grains—such as potatoes, corn, rice, barley, millet, and quinoa—the principal role in meals. This is what the majority of the world's population has done for thousands of years. Standard vegetarian fare such as pasta with sauce or stir-fried vegetables with rice are examples of how we intuitively integrated this concept into North American cuisine.

The sauce and dressing recipes in this book were designed to be used on conventional salads as well your own grain and vegetable combinations. Be innovative! Consider the recipes as a starting point; then let your creativity and personal expression transport you and your taste buds to new and exciting realms. Adjust the recipes as you see fit, according to your individual preferences or what is in your pantry. Alternatively, use them as a guide for developing your own original no-cook sauces and dressings.

How to Use This Book

This book is really several in one. It is:

➤ a source book for devising imaginative vegetarian meals;

➤ a reference for improvising your own special creations;

➤ and, of course, a book of recipes for every kind of savory no-cook sauce and dressing imaginable.

Use each section as an independent manual, or as a means to steer you through the process of preparing grain-centered vegetarian meals and inspired sauces and dressings.

Special Equipment

If you have a well-equipped kitchen, you should have no difficulty preparing any of the sauce or dressing recipes in this book. Standard measuring spoons, measuring cups, cutting boards, and mixing bowls are indispensable. A blender and food processor are the only special appliances you'll need; however, a powerful, sturdy blender may be able to stand in for a food processor in many cases. If your blender does a reasonable job mixing thick sauces and dressings, and you don't own a food processor, I wouldn't encourage you to make an unnecessary purchase. A food processor, on the other hand, cannot substitute for the pulverizing capability of a blender. For some recipes, a blender is absolutely essential to achieve a smooth or creamy consistency. Recipes that don't call for blending or processing may simply be whisked together in a small bowl.

Additional Helpful Equipment

➢ *Citrus juicer/reamer* – The bright, lively flavor of freshly squeezed lemon, lime, and orange juice is always preferable to the stale, flat liquid found in canned, bottled, or frozen products. A variety of citrus juicers and reamers are available in cookware stores, and most do an excellent job. Hand-held and counter-top reamers require a bit more elbow grease to extract the juice than electric models, but the extra effort is nicely rewarded with a high yield.

➢ *Garlic press* – This wonderful gadget makes fast work of mincing fresh garlic. For the easiest cleanup, look for a garlic press with an integrated cleaning device. If you are regularly short on time, purchase crushed garlic in a jar and store it in the refrigerator. It's almost as flavorful as fresh garlic and very convenient.

➢ *Ginger grater* – This small, ceramic or stainless steel grater has fine, sharp teeth for rapidly shredding the gnarly fibers of fresh gingerroot. If you choose to make recipes calling for fresh ginger juice (see page 137), this tool is a necessity.

➢ *Pepper mill* – Freshly ground pepper has a pungency and bite that is far superior to the taste of packaged ground pepper. Select a mill with grinding adjustments from fine to coarse.

➢ *Rubber spatulas* – Flexible rubber spatulas are indispensable for scraping every last bit of sauce or dressing from your blender, food processor, or mixing bowl.

➢ *Storage containers* – Glass jars and plastic storage containers with snug fitting lids are essential for storing your homemade sauces and dressings in the refrigerator.

➢ *Wire whisk* – A whisk speedily blends ingredients much more efficiently than a fork or spoon. Two sizes are helpful: a medium-size whisk to use in mixing bowls, and a mini-whisk that's small enough to use in measuring cups.

➢ *Zester* – A zester is a small kitchen gadget with a short, flat blade that has a beveled edge containing five small holes. Draw it over the skin of a lemon, lime, or orange to remove long, thin strips of the colored rind. (Note: Avoid zesting the white part of the fruit just below the colored skin as this is very bitter.)

Planning Vegetarian Meals

Many people have difficulty planning vegetarian menus or get stuck in a cycle of preparing the same foods over and over. An easy, economical, exciting, and versatile way to organize vegetarian meals is to center them around whole grains or starches.

Following is a 1-2-3 summary and an itemized chart for tailoring vegetarian meals to suit your own individual needs and tastes.

❶ Select rice, whole grain, pasta, or potatoes as the center of your meal. Choose a fat-free or nearly fat-free style of cooking (steaming, simmering, pressure-cooking, or baking).

❷ Select essential accompaniments, which include plenty of fresh, uncooked or lightly cooked vegetables, and optional accompaniments, which include cooked beans, tempeh, tofu, or seitan.

❸ Select an optional dressing or sauce, choosing from the wide array of recipes in this book. Alternatively, invent your own special topping by following the guidelines on pages 34 through 40.

The Custom Designed Vegetarian Meal

Grains or Starches *choose 1*	Raw or Cooked Vegetables *choose 2 or more* (incorporate a variety of contrasting colors)	Protein Additions *choose 1* (optional)	No-Cook Sauce or Dressings *choose 1* (optional)
Bread, whole-grain (e.g. whole wheat chapatis, cornbread, pita bread, yeast bread, baked tortillas) ✳ Grains, whole (e.g. barley, brown rice, bulgur, corn, millet, quinoa, wild rice) ✳ Grains, refined (e.g. couscous, white rice) ✳ Pasta ✳ Potatoes, white, gold, red, blue ✳ Potatoes, yams/sweets ✳ Squash, hard-shell winter* *Winter squash is dense and satisfying. Served in larger portions, it can form the foundation of a meal. Or it can be used as a vegetable addition to grains or starches.*	Dark leafy greens (e.g. chard, collards, kale, mustard, spinach) ✳ Other green vegetables (e.g. asparagus, broccoli, bok choy, Brussels sprouts, cabbage, green peppers, green beans) ✳ Orange/yellow vegetables (e.g. carrots, rutabaga, squash, yellow peppers, wax beans) ✳ Red or purple vegetables (e.g. beets, red bell peppers, red cabbage, tomatoes) ✳ Ivory/tan vegetables (e.g. cauliflower, celeriac, fennel, kohlrabi, mushrooms, parsnips, turnips) ✳ Lettuce and tender salad greens ✳ Miscellaneous vegetables (e.g. celery, cucumbers, eggplant, leeks, onions, radishes, scallions, zucchini)	Beans ✳ Lentils ✳ Meat substitutes ✳ Peas ✳ Tempeh ✳ Tofu ✳ Seitan	Bean-based sauce or dressing ✳ Fat-free sauce or dressing ✳ Nut-based sauce or dressing ✳ Oil and vinegar dressing ✳ Seed-based sauce or dressing ✳ Tofu-based sauce or dressing ✳ Tomato-based sauce or dressing

Putting It All Together

✳ Sample Menus

Baked winter squash stuffed with
wild and brown rice
Steamed collard greens
Kidney beans
or sautéed tempeh strips
Umeboshi and Herb Dressing, p. 52

✳

Bow-tie pasta
Steamed broccoli florets
Steamed, diagonally sliced carrots
Julienned red bell pepper strips
Plain or seasoned tofu cubes
Michael's Red Dressing, p. 50

✳

Baked sweet potatoes
Steamed kale
Sliced cooked beets
Dried or frozen lima beans, cooked
Del Sol Dressing, p. 45

✳

Bulgur
Steamed beet greens or Swiss chard
Steamed julienned carrots
Diced cooked beets
Hummus Sauce, p. 100

✳

Corkscrew pasta
Fresh asparagus, cut into
1-inch pieces, steamed tender-crisp
Oil-packed sun-dried tomatoes,
drained and thinly sliced
Fennel-Mustard Sauce, p. 55

Millet
Shredded red cabbage
Steamed cauliflower florets
I Can't Believe It's Not Cheese
Sauce, p. 87
Sliced scallions (for garnish)

✳

Cooked chick-peas
Halved cherry tomatoes
Thinly sliced red or black
radishes
Thinly sliced English cucumber
Torn romaine lettuce
Sesame-Orange Vinaigrette,
p. 61
Whole-grain rolls or cornbread

✳

Steamed or boiled red potatoes
Steamed green beans
Creamy Pesto Sauce, p. 110

✳

Basmati rice
Steamed mixed vegetables
Fresh or frozen green peas, cooked
Thai Hot and Sour Dressing, p. 81

✳

Whole-wheat couscous
Cooked red kidney beans
Diced fresh tomato
Fresh or frozen corn, thawed
Minced green bell pepper
Chili Lime Dressing, p. 47

Tips for a Perfect Presentation

➤ Be sure to vary the colors and textures of the foods you are serving. Visual appeal is essential to the presentation of all fine foods. Contrasting colors and textures contribute greatly to the beauty of meals, regardless of the complexity or simplicity of the individual ingredients. This practice also adds to the healthfulness of meals by compelling the cook to incorporate a wide variety of foods.

➤ Provide an assortment of tastes, and try not to repeat flavors or present analogous foods at the same meal (e.g. don't serve a bean-based sauce over beans). Minimize fat by using a fat-free or low-fat sauce or dressing, and refrain from serving nuts, seeds, avocado, or other high-fat ingredients when including a sauce or dressing rich in oil or vegetable fat.

➤ Garnishes add distinction and panache to dishes and require nothing more than a light shower of fresh herbs; a dusting of paprika or freshly ground black pepper; a sprinkle of thinly sliced scallion; a scattering of finely minced or shredded raw vegetables (such as radish, carrot, or zucchini); or artfully strewn chopped nuts or seeds (raw or toasted). Olives, lemon slices, tomato wedges, and capers make handy, uncomplicated final touches. Present garnishes in uneven numbers— for instance, 1, 3, or 5 of an item instead of 2 or 4—for greater interest and allure.

Presentation Options

➤ Present each part of the meal autonomously, using a single sauce or dressing on all items to create a sense of unity. Alternatively, use several different sauces or dressings to accentuate the uniqueness of each item on the menu, or use a sauce or dressing on one item only.

➤ Toss some or all of the items together salad-style, combined with a sauce or dressing of your choice. Alternatively, serve the sauce or dressing on the side.

➤ Layer the items in tiers, drizzled with a sauce or dressing, or serve a sauce or dressing on the side.

Nearly all the sauce and dressing recipes in this book take no longer than 5 minutes to prepare. Therefore, the duration of your meal preparation will revolve around the item that takes the longest time to cook. In most instances, this will be a rice, grain, or other starch. When you are extremely pressed for time, prepare a quick-cooking refined grain like couscous (6 minutes), white basmati rice (10 minutes), pasta (7 minutes), steamed potato chunks (12 minutes), or steamed winter squash halves (15 minutes). On days when you can cook at a more leisurely pace, prepare longer-cooking items like brown rice, baked potatoes, or dried beans. Occasionally, plan ahead to make larger quantities than will be consumed at a single sitting in order to use them for lunches or dinners throughout the week.

The worksheet on the next page will help you keep track of the memorable dishes you create so you can easily make them again. Feel free to make copies of this worksheet, and keep plenty on hand.

Worksheet for Creative Meal Planning

Grain or Starch   **Amount**

_____   _____

Cooking Liquid   **Amount**

_____   _____

Cooking Method   **Time**

_____   _____

Seasonings

_____   _____

Oil _____

Salt _____

Herbs/Spices _____

Vegetables (raw or cooked)

_____

_____

_____

_____

Protein Accompaniments

_____

No-Cook Sauce or Dressing

_____

Garnish

_____

Presentation ___ autonomous   ___ salad-style   ___ layered
                 ___ combination of styles

Notes

_____

_____

_____

_____

The Six Basic Tastes

There are six basic taste sensations in the different foods we eat:

* **Sweet**   * **Sour**

* **Salty**   * **Pungent**

* **Bitter**   * **Astringent**

In most recipes or combinations of foods that make up a meal these tastes are intermixed to varying degrees. The measure of an outstanding meal and an exemplary sauce or dressing is an impeccable and imperceptible balance of these flavors.

Many foods and seasonings we enjoy contain two or more of these tastes. For instance, almonds are sweet and bitter; parsley is pungent, bitter, and astringent; and garlic combines all of the tastes except sour. Gaining an appreciation of these tastes and how they harmonize with each other will help you to create exceptional no-cook sauces and dressings and devise delicious, imaginative meals.

Sweet

All sweeteners are included in this category, but many other foods are naturally sweet as well. Sweet foods include most fruits, certain vegetables (such as sweet potatoes and squash), and items that are mostly carbohydrate (such as pasta and bread), protein (such as tofu and lentils), or fat (such as avocado, nuts, and oil).

Sour

Sour foods are those which are tangy, tart, and acidic, or are rendered acidic through fermentation. Examples of foods in this category include citrus fruits, tomatoes, vinegar, and sauerkraut.

Salty

Salt stimulates digestion and also makes our mouths water. Although table salt is the most common form, salt is present in many other foods including Bragg Liquid Aminos, fermented foods such as soy sauce and miso, and pickled foods such as sauerkraut and umeboshi plums.

Pungent

Pungent foods and seasonings are those which heat up our tongue and mouth and, in larger quantities, make us feel warm or flushed. Chiles, garlic, ginger, horseradish, mustard, and pepper are all examples of widely-used pungent seasonings.

Bitter

Bitter foods have a sharp or biting edge to them. Green leafy vegetables are included in this category, as are chocolate, coffee, tea, almonds, walnuts, and many medicinal herbs.

Astringent

Astringent foods are best defined as those which make us pucker by causing the tissues of our mouth to contract. These foods have a cleansing, toning, or tightening effect on the palate. Good examples are lemons and cranberries. Not all sour foods are astringent, however, and not all astringent foods are sour. Examples of non-sour astringent foods are apples, beans, broccoli, lentils, potatoes, quinoa, and sage.

General Taste Guidelines for Various Foods

- **Legumes**—All legumes (peas, beans, and lentils) and products made from them (such as tofu and tempeh) are both sweet and astringent.

- **Grains**—All rices and grains and products made from them (such as bread and pasta) are sweet. Couscous, quinoa, rye, spelt, triticale, and wheat are both sweet and astringent.

- **Nuts and Seeds**—All nuts and seeds are sweet. Almonds, tahini, sunflower seeds, and walnuts are both sweet and bitter. Peanuts, which are a legume, are both sweet and astringent.

- **Oils**—All oils are sweet. Flax oil and safflower oil are both sweet and pungent.

- **Vinegars**—All vinegars are sour. Umeboshi plum vinegar is both sour and salty. Balsamic vinegar is both sour and sweet.

Taste Chart

Vegetable	Taste
Artichokes	sweet, astringent
Asparagus	sweet, bitter, astringent
Beets	sweet, bitter
Bell Peppers	sweet, astringent
Broccoli	bitter, astringent
Brussels Sprouts	sweet, bitter, astringent
Cabbage	sweet, astringent
Carrots	sweet, pungent
Cauliflower	sweet, astringent
Celery	sweet, bitter, astringent
Collard Greens	bitter, astringent
Corn	sweet
Cucumbers	sweet, astringent
Eggplant	bitter
Fennel	pungent
Garlic	all except sour
Green Beans	sweet, astringent
Kale	bitter, astringent
Lettuce	bitter, astringent
Mushrooms	sweet, astringent
Mustard Greens	pungent, bitter
Okra	sweet
Onions (chives, scallions, leeks, and shallots)	sweet, pungent
Parsnips	sweet
Potatoes	astringent
Radishes	bitter
Rutabagas	astringent
Sea Vegetables	salty, astringent
Spinach and Swiss Chard	bitter
Squash (winter and summer)	sweet
Sweet Potatoes	sweet
Tomatoes	sweet, sour
Turnips	astringent

Fruit	Taste
Apples	sweet, astringent
Apricots	sweet, sour
Avocados	sweet
Bananas	sweet, astringent
Blueberries	sweet, astringent
Cranberries	sweet, astringent
Cherries	sweet, sour
Currants	sweet
Dates	sweet
Figs	sweet, astringent
Grapefruits	sour
Grapes	sweet, sour
Kiwi	sweet, sour
Lemons	sour, astringent
Limes	sour
Mangoes	sweet, sour
Melons	sweet
Nectarines	sweet, sour
Oranges	sweet, sour
Papayas	sweet
Peaches	sweet, sour
Pears	sweet
Persimmons	sweet, astringent
Pineapples	sweet, sour
Plums	sweet, sour
Pomegranates	sweet, sour, astringent
Raisins	sweet
Raspberries/Blackberries	sweet, sour
Strawberries	sweet, sour, astringent
Tangerines	sweet, sour

Taste Chart

Herbs, Spices & Seasonings	Taste
Allspice	pungent
Basil	pungent
Bragg Liquid Aminos	salty, astringent
Caraway	pungent
Cilantro	pungent
Cinnamon	pungent, bitter
Coriander	pungent, bitter
Cumin	pungent
Curry Powder	pungent, bitter, astringent
Dill Weed	pungent
Fennel	pungent
Ginger	sweet, pungent
Horseradish	pungent
Lemon/Orange Zest	bitter
Marjoram	pungent
Mint	pungent
Mirin	sweet, sour
Miso (sweet white)	sweet, salty

Herbs, Spices & Seasonings	Taste
Mustard, dry	pungent
Mustard, prepared	sour, salty, pungent
Nutmeg	pungent, astringent
Nutritional Yeast	bitter
Oregano	pungent
Paprika	pungent
Parsley	pungent, astringent
Pepper (black, white, cayenne)	pungent
Poppy Seeds	sweet, pungent, astringent
Rosemary	pungent, bitter, astringent
Sage	pungent, astringent
Tamari Soy Sauce	sweet, salty
Tarragon	pungent
Thyme	pungent
Turmeric	pungent, bitter, astringent
Umeboshi Plums	sour, salty

Components of No-Cook Sauces & Dressings

The Role of Fats & Oils

Quick and easy cooking techniques such as steaming, steam-frying, and baking are especially appealing to today's health-conscious cooks because they lock in the nutrients in food and do not require added fat. Cooking without fat is not only better for your health, it makes cleanup much easier as well.

Although low-fat and no-fat cooking methods are highly recommended, many of the sauces and dressings in this book do contain some fat in the form of oil, nut or seed butter, avocado, or tofu. Small amounts of fat can be valuable in sauces and dressings because they carry and amplify flavor, add richness and body, and provide a physical as well as psychological sense of satisfaction.

Vegetable oils and high-fat plant foods vary considerably, all having their own distinct flavor, color, aroma, mouth feel, and textural properties. Most vegetable oils and other dense forms of vegetable fat contribute, on the average, approximately 100 to 130 calories and 7 to 16 grams of fat per tablespoon. Therefore, it's a good idea to limit the amount of oil or fat used in a recipe or restrict the serving size of recipes containing high-fat ingredients. *Moderation,* not elimination, is the key. The sauce and dressing recipes in this book were specifically devised to be high in flavor, so even though they may contain vegetable oil or other high-fat plant ingredients, a little will go a long way in seasoning a dish.

Modern oil production consists of many unhealthful processes including hexane solvent extraction, degumming, bleaching, and deodorizing. Temperatures can range from 130°F to over 500°F for durations of 30 to 60 minutes, which can change the oil's chemical composition and transform it from healthful to harmful. The finest cooking and salad oils are those that are less refined. Most natural food stores and many supermarkets carry a range of oils that have been mechanically extracted in an expeller press, which circumvents the need for a chemical solvent.

Although somewhat of a misnomer, the term "cold pressed" merely means that the oils have not been exposed to the degree of heat that destroys essential fatty acids and certain nutrients. These unrefined oils, which are pressed at lower temperatures, retain valuable nutritional elements and also carry the flavor of the seed, nut, or fruit from which they were pressed. Look for oils that are labeled "expeller pressed" and "unrefined." It is also wise to seek out organic oils whenever possible. Although higher in price, the taste, quality, and healthfulness of unrefined, expeller-pressed, organic oils make them well worth the extra expense. And, by incorporating them into sauces and dressings where they will not be heated or cooked, you are safeguarding your purchase as well as your health.

Some vegetable oils and other plant sources of fat impart body and texture to sauces and dressings without contributing much in the way of taste. Canola oil, safflower oil, and silken tofu are examples of "background" ingredients. Light-flavored oils and mild-tasting tofu are best to use when a blander flavor is desired or when a bolder taste would compete with other elements. Extra-virgin olive oil and pure nut or seed oils—such as walnut oil, hazelnut oil, and sesame oil—are well-suited to no-cook sauces and dressings and add delicate but distinctive undertones. They can be quite costly and are prone to turning rancid quickly, so buy them in small quantities and refrigerate them as soon as possible.

Edible "whole" plant fats are obtained from fruits, legumes, nuts, and seeds, each having its own unique color, aroma, and flavor. Examples of high-fat plant foods include walnuts, sesame seeds, olives, peanuts, soybeans, and avocadoes. They are considered a natural source of fat because their oil is not extracted out; the whole food is used instead. These whole, high-fat plant foods and products made from them—such as nut butter and tofu—add a sumptuous texture as well as characteristic flavor. When you think of them as substitutes for oil, a wide array of new possibilities can emerge.

Nuts, seeds, and the butters made from them are rich in fiber and protein as well as fat. Natural nut and seed butters do not use hydrogenated oil as an emulsifier (as do most supermarket brands). They therefore need to be stirred after opening to distribute the oil that separates out and rises to the top. Alternatively, this oil may be poured off, resulting in a slightly drier butter. (This oil can be incorporated into sauces or dressings or used for cooking.) Refrigerating the nut or seed butter after stirring will retard the oil from separating out again. In addition to traditional peanut butter, natural food stores carry a range of delicious nut and seed butters including cashew, hazelnut, almond, pecan, pistachio, macadamia, sesame, sunflower, and others. For the best nutrition and flavor, always choose natural butters made from organically grown nuts and seeds whenever possible.

Tofu is considered by some to be a high-fat product because, compared to most other legumes except peanuts, soybeans (from which tofu is made) are rich in oil. Most of the recipes in this book that require tofu call for *silken* tofu, also known as Japanese tofu. One such brand is Mori-Nu, a readily available product that imparts a rich, creamy texture. Their "lite" silken tofu is ideal for no-cook sauces and dressings because this reduced-fat product is velvety and luscious and produces a rich-tasting result that is imperceptible from its full-fat counterpart.

Mori-Nu tofu is packed in aseptic boxes so it will keep for a long time and doesn't need to be refrigerated until the package is opened. If you choose to use another brand, be sure to select a Japanese-style tofu that is soft and creamy in order to create smooth-textured sauces and dressings. Most water-packed tofu is Chinese-style, a more coarsely textured product that is better suited for stir-frying, marinating, and grilling.

Storing Oils & Nut or Seed Butters

Less refined oils and fats in the form of nut and seed butters are prone to becoming rancid quicker than more highly refined products. Light and air induce the breakdown of their nutritional composition, so it is essential that these relatively unrefined products be refrigerated before and after opening. Some oils, such as olive oil and sauces or dressings made from it, may turn cloudy or even solidify when chilled. However, they will become clear and liquefy again when brought to room temperature.

Purchase oils and nut or seed butters in small quantities and mark the date of purchase on their labels. Look for oils packaged in opaque containers—metal, dark glass, earthenware, or plastic. Although dark glass lets in some light rays, it is better than clear glass. Oils sold in most supermarkets are highly refined and are rarely available in anything except clear glass or plastic. Unrefined oils in opaque containers are sold at natural food stores.

Most oils will keep for four to six months and nut or seed butters for about one month when stored in the refrigerator. For slightly longer storage, oils and nut and seed butters may be kept in the freezer. Oils will not freeze solidly, so they do not need to be defrosted before using. Test oils and nut or seed butters for rancidity before using them if they have been stored longer than these periods. Rancid oils and butters taste bitter and cause a burning sensation at the back of the throat. They may also have an "off," unpleasant, or strong odor.

Reducing Fat & Oil

The easiest way to create a low-fat or no-fat sauce or dressing is simply to leave out the oil and substitute an equal amount of water or vegetable stock. The result will be a thinner sauce or dressing, but the flavor should be intact.

For a slightly thicker dressing, a starch and water mixture may be used to replace part or all of the oil. Place 1 cup *cool* water (to prevent clumping) and 1 tablespoon + 1 teaspoon arrowroot, kuzu, or cornstarch in a small saucepan. Whisk them together until the starch is well dissolved. Bring to a simmer over medium heat and cook, stirring constantly, until the mixture is clear and thickened. Cool, then store in the refrigerator. The mixture will keep for about seven days.

Dressings and sauces that incorporate nuts, seeds, nut or seed butters, olives, or avocado *require* these ingredients to achieve a particular taste and consistency. Nevertheless, these ingredients may be reduced by one-quarter to one-half and replaced with an equal amount of lite silken tofu without dramatically affecting the recipe's outcome. Keep in mind that silken tofu will produce a creamier sauce or dressing with a lighter color and taste. It also requires blending in order to obtain a smooth consistency.

Thinning thick dressings made with high-fat ingredients is yet another easy way to reduce the fat and calorie content. (See page 39.) Sauces and dressings in this book were designed to be on the thick side, so many can be thinned with no loss of flavor or appeal.

Recommended Oils

➤ **Dark sesame oil** (also called *Chinese* or *Japanese sesame oil* or *toasted sesame oil*) is made from roasted sesame seeds, giving the oil an amber color and a fabulous rich flavor and aroma. Sesame oil made from unroasted seeds is called "light" or "European" sesame oil. It is golden in color with a more subtle yet still clear sesame taste. Dark sesame oil used in small amounts in no-cook sauces and dressings contributes a luscious, exotic flavor. Hot chile oil (also called *hot pepper oil* or *red oil*) is dark sesame oil infused with spicy red chile peppers. It is usually fiery hot and therefore should be used sparingly.

➤ **Expeller-pressed canola oil and high-oleic safflower oil** (high in monounsaturated fat) have a mild taste and are suitable for use alone or in combination with olive oil to produce a lighter-tasting dressing or sauce. These oils are ideal for recipes where blandness is desirable or where olive oil or other strong-tasting oils would overpower delicate flavors.

➤ **Extra-virgin olive oil** is one of the least processed oils. It is high in monounsaturated fat and also has an exceptional flavor. Cold pressing produces the best olive oil because it yields a naturally low level of acidity. "Extra-virgin" means the oil is the result of the first pressing of the olives and is only one percent acid. It is the finest and fruitiest of the olive oils and consequently the most expensive. Extra-virgin olive oil ranges in color from amber champagne to greenish-golden to bright green. In general, the deeper the color the more intense the olive flavor. "Pure olive oil" and "olive oil" are produced from the second or third pressings of the same olives used to make extra-virgin oil. They are generally much paler in color with a weak olive flavor and a very oily taste. Don't be fooled by olive oil labeled "light" —it has the same fat and calories as regular olive oil. What the term "light" refers to is the lighter color and fragrance and nondescript flavor resulting from an extremely fine filtration process. If you can't smell the olives, don't use the oil!

➤ *Flaxseed oil* is an abundant source of omega-3 fatty acids, one of the essential fatty acids most often lacking in modern diets. Omega-3 fatty acids have been attributed with amazing healing and disease preventive properties and improving the health and appearance of skin, hair, and nails. Adding flax oil to no-cook sauces and dressings is perhaps the easiest and most nutritious way to incorporate this essential fatty acid into your daily diet.

Because flax oil is prone to rancidity and highly susceptible to nutrient loss from exposure to air, light, and heat, special care must be taken when purchasing, storing, and using it. Always keep flax oil in the refrigerator. Recap it immediately after use and return it to the refrigerator as soon as possible. *Never heat flax oil or use it in cooking or baking.* Purchase only refrigerated flax oil in small quantities. It should come packaged in a light-impervious plastic or dark glass bottle that is stamped with a freshness date. Use it up within two to three weeks after opening the bottle or by the freshness date. Storing flax oil in the freezer will extend its life a few weeks longer.

Flax oil has an assertive nutty taste that can sometimes over-power other flavors. The best way to add flax oil to your diet is to substitute it for one-quarter to one-half of the oil in no-cook sauce and dressing recipes, or, if you prefer its robust flavor, you can substitute even more. For sauce and dressing recipes that do not call for oil, and for those that use nut or seed butter, avocado, or olives as a foundation, flax oil may be added to the recipe one teaspoon at a time. Taste and see how the flavor appeals to you; then add a little more, if you like. If time permits, let your sauce or dressing rest briefly before serving; the taste of the flax oil will mellow as it blends with other flavors.

➤ *Hazelnut oil* is a versatile specialty oil with a splendid sophisticated flavor and light aroma that imparts substance and richness to all types of no-cook sauces and dressings.

➤ *Walnut oil* is a delicate, light-colored specialty oil with a distinct walnut flavor and slightly bitter taste. It is high in polyunsaturated fatty acids and has a slightly longer shelf life than flaxseed oil.

Recommended Nut & Seed Butters

➤ **Almond butter** is made from either raw or roasted nuts. Raw almond butter is mild and light in color. Roasted almond butter has a richer flavor and a deep brown color. Almond butter is available in both smooth and crunchy styles. Even the smooth style usually leaves a few nutty pieces in sauces and dressings, adding a bit of texture.

➤ **Cashew butter** is made from either raw or roasted cashews and has a high fat content which makes it creamy and smooth. Raw cashew butter is sweet and mild with a light tan color. It makes a delicate, no-cook cream sauce or sumptuous cream dressing when combined with water and seasonings. Roasted cashew butter has a deeper brown color and a more intense nutty flavor.

➤ **Peanut butter** is the most common and well-loved of all nut butters. It comes in two styles—crunchy and smooth—and has a strong, deep roasted flavor. Consistency, taste, and texture of natural peanut butter varies among manufacturers. Purchase *only* organically grown peanut butters that have nothing added except perhaps salt. Non-organically grown peanut crops are customarily rotated with cotton crops which are routinely treated with highly toxic chemicals that leach into the soil. Furthermore, peanuts are prone to a carcinogenic mold called *aflatoxin*, which is prolific in peanuts harvested and stored in the humid areas of southeastern United States. Peanuts grown and stored in the arid Southwest are generally not tainted with aflatoxin. Walnut Acres regularly tests their organically produced peanut butters for aflatoxin. Other brands of peanut butter—such as some lines produced by Arrowhead Mills and Westbrae—are made from peanuts grown in New Mexico, so there is less chance of aflatoxin contamination.

➤ **Specialty nut and seed butters** are available in jars or in the bulk section of many natural food stores and food co-operatives. Among those you may find are hazelnut butter, macadamia butter, pecan butter, pine nut butter, pistachio butter, sesame butter (a thick, deeply roasted version of tahini), and sunflower butter.

Each of these has a unique flavor and consistency and is worth the occasional indulgence if you enjoy the sophisticated, somewhat exotic tastes they impart to no-cook sauces and dressings. Because these specialty butters can be somewhat expensive, purchase them in small quantities, especially when you are first trying them out.

➤ *Tahini* is made by grinding raw or lightly toasted whole or hulled sesame seeds. It is light tan in color and makes a rich and creamy, slightly bitter base for no-cook sauces and dressings. The consistency of tahini varies from brand to brand with some being creamy and smooth and others being oily or dry. Seek out tahini made from organically grown sesame seeds for the best flavor and quality.

The Role of Vinegars & Acidulants

Vinegar (which is a diluted acid), citrus juice (such as lemon, lime, orange, and grapefruit), and brine (from pickled products such as sauerkraut, pickles, and olives) add piquant tartness to savory no-cook sauces and dressings. These acidulants act as natural preservatives, retarding the growth of bacteria. They each impart a particular flavor in addition to acidity and contribute virtually no calories.

Vinegar has been used for centuries for a variety of applications. The word "vinegar" was derived from the French term *vin aigre*, which means "sour wine." Like wine, vinegar is produced through natural fermentation, is highly aromatic, and comes in a wide range of hues and flavors. Store vinegar in a cool, dark place. Most vinegars will keep two years or longer unopened. Once opened, write the date on the bottle and store it for about six months, preferably in the refrigerator.

Recommended Vinegars & Acidulants

➤ *Apple cider vinegar* is an extremely tart, fruity vinegar made from fermented apple cider. "Raw" apple cider vinegar is made the traditional way by aging the cider at least six months in cypress and cedar casks.

➤ *Balsamic vinegar* is an exquisitely flavored seasoning made from white Trebbiano grape juice that acquires a dark amber color and pungent sweetness after aging for three to thirty years in barrels made from various woods—red oak, chestnut, mulberry, and juniper. The finest balsamics are slightly sweet, heavy, mellow, and dark.

➤ *Brine* from olives, sauerkraut, and pickles can be used alone or in combination with other acidic ingredients—such as vinegar or lemon juice—to impart a special pungency and tartness. Brine also can be used as a salt seasoning in no-cook sauces and dressings, and adds beneficial enzymes because of the fermentation process it has undergone.

➤ *Brown rice vinegar* is a mild acidulant made from fermented brown rice. It is widely used in Japanese and Chinese cooking and adds a light, exotic flavor to sauces and dressings. Traditionally, the vinegar is brewed in earthenware crocks. It is then filtered and aged in casks until the flavor is mellow and the color is deep amber.

➤ *Citrus juices*, most often lemon and lime juice, are commonly used in place of vinegar in many dressings and no-cook sauces. Lime juice is slightly less sharp than lemon juice, but the two can usually be used interchangeably. Orange juice adds a gentle tartness to sauces and dressings, while grapefruit juice adds a spirited bite. Always use freshly squeezed citrus juice. Canned, bottled, reconstituted, and frozen juices are unacceptable (except for frozen orange juice concentrate).

➤ *Fruit vinegars* are made by blending soft fruits—such as raspberries, blueberries, or peaches—and/or fruit concentrates with a mild vinegar. Sugar and/or fruit liqueurs are often added to enhance the flavor and offset the vinegar's acidity.

➤ *Herbal vinegars* are made by soaking one or several different kinds of herbs in white or red wine vinegar or apple cider vinegar.

➤ *Umeboshi plums* are a salty Japanese seasoning made from whole Japanese plums, an herb called beefsteak leaf (*red shiso*), and sea salt. This pickle is then fermented for a minimum of eighteen months resulting in a condiment that is at once salty and sour with a deep fuschia color. Although some cooks store whole umeboshi plums at room temperature, refrigeration is recommended. They will keep for several months.

➢ *Umeboshi plum paste* is the mashed meat of umeboshi plums. (See previous page.) This convenient seasoning paste must be diluted for even distribution in no-cook sauces and dressings. Store it in a tightly sealed container in the refrigerator. It will keep for several months.

➢ *Umeboshi plum vinegar* is a bright purple-pink vinegar made from the liquid used to pickle umeboshi plums. (See previous page.) It has a gloriously intense tart flavor and a strong salty taste. Umeboshi plum vinegar can be used as an acidulant as well as a salt seasoning in dressings and no-cook sauces.

➢ *Wine vinegar* is the most popular acidulant used in salad dressings. It is produced from the acetic fermentation of red or white wine and retains much of the wine's mellow flavor and aroma.

The Role of Salt Seasonings

Salt, used prudently, enhances the flavor of no-cook sauces and dressings and can harmonize an array of isolated flavors. Used with awareness and intention, salt is a magical seasoning. The concern with too much salt in the diet stems primarily from an overconsumption of processed foods. Manufacturers rely heavily on salt (as well as fat and sugar) to achieve an element of flavor in drastically denatured, non-nutritive products. If you limit consumption of processed foods, you will immediately reduce your intake of salt. You can then use salt judiciously as a cooking aid to draw out the natural flavors of whole foods and balance other seasonings. Most chefs consider salt an essential flavoring ingredient. However, many people on salt-restricted diets discover that a little extra lemon juice and/or other acidic ingredients offsets the need for salt in dressings and no-cook sauces.

It's valuable to expand the concept of salt seasonings beyond plain salt to include salty foods and condiments such as naturally brewed soy sauce (*tamari* and *shoyu*) or Liquid Aminos, umeboshi plums (and umeboshi paste and vinegar), miso, and fermented foods such as olives, sauerkraut, and their brine. When including these salty seasonings, be sure to reduce or eliminate added salt, letting your taste buds lead the way.

Recommended Salt Seasonings

➤ **Bragg Liquid Aminos** is a soy sauce-like condiment, but unlike soy sauce, Bragg Liquid Aminos is not fermented. Its flavor is complex and wine-like. Although it is very salty tasting, it contains no added salt. Bragg Liquid Aminos is made by extracting amino acids from organic soybeans, and the salty flavor comes solely from the natural sodium found in the soybeans. In addition to being salty, Bragg Liquid Aminos is also astringent. Store Bragg Liquid Aminos at room temperature. It will keep indefinitely.

➤ **Miso** is a salty Japanese condiment, prized for its healthful enzymes which are said to aid digestion. It is traditionally made with water, soybeans, salt, a fermented rice called *koji*, and a grain such as barley or rice. Misos come in a tremendous variety of colors and tastes, not unlike fine wine. The lighter the miso, the sweeter and less salty it will be. I particularly recommend sweet white miso for use in no-cook sauces and dressings because of its tantalizing yet delicate flavor. Since miso is a paste, it must be diluted for even distribution in no-cook sauces and dressings. For the best flavor, purchase unpasteurized miso (it will be in the refrigerated section of your natural foods store) instead of pasteurized miso sold in vacuum-sealed packages. Store miso in a tightly sealed container in the refrigerator. It will keep for several months.

➤ **Naturally brewed soy sauce (*tamari and shoyu*)** is produced by the natural fermentation of soybeans, salt, water, and sometimes wheat. Naturally brewed soy sauce is called *shoyu* if wheat is used, *tamari* if it is not. The finest soy sauces are aged for a year or longer. With time, you will develop as discriminating a taste for tamari and shoyu as some people have for fine wine. Store tamari or shoyu at room temperature or in the refrigerator for optimum flavor. It will keep indefinitely.

➤ **Olives and olive paste (mashed or blended olives)** contribute both oil and salt seasoning, while the **olive brine** can be used as an acidulant and/or salt seasoning.

➤ **Sauerkraut and sauerkraut juice** can be used as salt seasonings. Each has a distinct sour and salty taste similar to umeboshi. Purchase sauerkraut that is made with only cabbage and salt.

For salt-restricted diets, low-sodium sauerkraut and its juice can, like lemon juice, often deceive the taste buds by imparting a salt-like flavor.

➤ *Seasoned salt* is regular table salt combined with other flavoring ingredients. Examples are onion salt, garlic salt, and celery salt, as well as salt blends with pulverized herbs, spices, and/or vegetables.

➤ *Umeboshi plums (and paste)* are Japanese plums that have been pickled with sea salt and an herb called beefsteak leaf (*red shiso*), and fermented for at least eighteen months. Umeboshi plums are a vibrant pink color and have a taste that is both salty and sour. In Japan, umeboshi plums and umeboshi plum paste (the mashed meat of the whole pitted plum) are served as a condiment, often with rice. They are also used as a digestive aid and as a medicinal for a wide range of ailments. Store umeboshi plums and paste in the refrigerator. They will keep for several months.

➤ *Umeboshi plum vinegar* is the extracted juices from the pickling of umeboshi plums. It has a bright pink color, the fruitiness of a fine wine, the tartness of fresh lemon juice, and a strong, salty flavor. It brings flat-tasting sauces and dressings to life, and adds the perfect balance to nut and seed butter-based recipes. It is the "secret ingredient" to reach for first.

The Role of Herbs & Spices

➤ *Herbs: The fragrant leaves of various annual and perennial plants and shrubs with non-woody stems.*

➤ *Spices: Pungent or aromatic seasonings obtained from the seeds, stems, buds, bark, roots, fruit, or flowers of a variety of plants and trees.*

Most people are hesitant to experiment with herbs and spices. Perhaps it's because we erroneously came to believe there is only one "right way" to combine seasonings. At one time, certain spices and herbs were confined to particular regions of the world. However, with modern transportation and immigration came an influx of new flavor sensations.

Actually, there are no rules for combining herbs and seasonings, whether they are fresh or dried. It's really what appeals to your own particular senses and taste that's important. Sample various seasonings to find out what appeals to you. Go to your local natural food store, co-op, or herb shop where dried herbs and spices are sold in bulk, and purchase small amounts of the ones you want to try. This way not only will you avoid paying for expensive packaging, you won't be stuck with large quantities of dried herbs and spices you don't like.

Although the possible combinations of herbs and spices are limitless, there are a few basic guidelines to be aware of. Don't use too many seasonings at once—usually one to three items per sauce or dressing is sufficient. Keep in mind the compatibility of the tastes (see page 14 for more information about the six tastes) and energetics of each seasoning. Energetics refers to the unique characteristics, temperament, and subtle attributes that distinguish each seasoning from another. It also refers to those traits that are held in common. The primary energetics of herbs and spices are:

* aromatic   * soothing
* stimulating

Dominant Herbs

Dominant herbs are those with flavors that overshadow others. These herbs work best when used as the primary seasoning. Examples of dominant herbs are:

* Cilantro   * Rosemary
* Dill weed   * Tarragon
* Mint

Complementary Herbs

Complementary herbs are those that work well when used in concert with other herbs. Examples of complementary herbs are:

* Basil   * Chives
* Fennel   * Oregano
* Parsley   * Thyme

The key to delicious flavor is to use the freshest seasonings possible. Dried leaf herbs, whole and ground spices, and seasoning blends are great—as long as they haven't been sitting on the pantry shelf for eons. Always store your dried herbs, spices, and any other seasonings in tightly sealed containers labeled with the date they were purchased. Whole spices will stay fresh for about two years; ground spices will stay fresh for about six months; and dried leaf herbs will stay fresh for about one year. Store the containers away from light, heat, and moisture (a cool, dry cupboard is best; not above the oven). And don't measure them out directly over a hot stove or steaming pot. Place them in a measuring spoon or in the palm of your hand first, then sprinkle them into the recipe. Most dried herbs should be crumbled with your fingers immediately before using them. This helps to release their aromatic oils and flavors. Certain herbs, such as dried thyme and rosemary, are brittle and will fare best if they are crushed just before using with a small mortar and pestle or in a small bowl using the back of a spoon.

Fresh herbs are highly perishable. To store them, cut off a small portion of the stems and immerse them in water, about one and a half inches deep. Then cover the leaves loosely with plastic wrap or a plastic bag, and store them in the refrigerator where they will keep for several days. To use fresh herbs, snip the leaves with kitchen shears or carefully break them off using your fingers just before you are ready to put the herbs in your recipe.

If a recipe calls for fresh herbs and you only have dried herbs on hand, use one teaspoon dried herb for each tablespoon (3 teaspoons) of fresh. Of course, if you have fresh herbs, you can substitute them in reverse by using about three times the amount of fresh herb for each quantity of dried herb required. When substituting ground herbs for dried leaf herbs, use about one-quarter to one-half the amount the recipe calls for.

To obtain the freshest flavor from dried spices, purchase a small spice grinder (available in natural food stores and cookware shops) and grind whole spices just before using them.

The Role of Sweeteners

When used in no-cook sauces and dressings, sweeteners temper the sharp edge of vinegars and other acidulants and help to round out and balance flavors.

Recommended Sweeteners

➤ *Agave nectar* is a natural liquid sweetener made from the core of the blue agave, a cactus-like plant native to Mexico, best known for its use in making tequila. It has a 93 percent fruit sugar content and is about 25 percent sweeter than sugar. Agave nectar dissolves easily and has a smooth, mild taste. Store tightly sealed at room temperature.

➤ *Apple juice and frozen apple juice concentrate* contribute a gentle, fruity sweetness to savory no-cook sauces and dressings. However, fruit overtones do not blend appealingly with every flavor or seasoning, so use this sweetener with discretion. Store in the refrigerator or freezer respectively.

➤ *Brown rice syrup* is a subtle sweetener made by combining cooked brown rice with dried, sprouted barley and culturing the mixture until malt enzymes convert some of the rice starch into glucose and maltose. Store tightly sealed at room temperature.

➤ *FruitSource* is a brand name sweetener made from grape juice concentrate and brown rice syrup and comes in both liquid and granular forms. It is delicious in its own right; however, it also makes an excellent substitute for honey, maple syrup, sugar, and other sweeteners. Store tightly sealed at room temperature.

➤ *Pure maple syrup* is a highly flavorful, concentrated sweetener. "Maple flavored syrup" consists primarily of sugar or corn syrup and usually contains artificial coloring and flavoring. Seek out only "pure maple syrup" for the finest quality. Grade AA will have the sweetest, most delicate flavor. The slightly thicker and darker grade B is better for baking. Some maple syrup processors use formaldehyde, chemical anti-foaming agents, and mold inhibitors. To ensure your maple syrup does not contain any of these, purchase only certified organic maple syrup and store it in the refrigerator.

➤ *Maple sugar* is made from dehydrated, crystallized maple syrup. Store maple sugar in an airtight container at room temperature.

➤ *Mirin* is a low-alcohol, slightly thick, Japanese white wine made from sweet glutinous rice. It imparts flavor as well as a delicate sweetness. Seek out naturally brewed mirin that does not contain added sugar. Once opened, mirin should be stored in the refrigerator.

➤ *Sorghum syrup* is a thick syrup made from the stalks of the sorghum plant, a cereal grain related to millet. Store sorghum syrup at room temperature during cooler seasons and in the refrigerator during warmer months to discourage insects and retard mold.

➤ *Sugar* is made from either sugarcane or beets. Unbleached cane sugars are slightly less refined and are sometimes organically grown. This group includes turbinado sugar, "raw" sugar, and a variety of brand name products, all of which are available in natural food stores and some supermarkets. These sweeteners retain more of the sugarcane's natural taste, color, and trace nutrients than are available in white table sugar. Some brands have fine golden crystals that easily dissolve and very closely resemble the taste and delicate texture of white table sugar. Other brands have deep amber-colored granules and a moderately strong molasses taste similar to brown sugar.

Developing Your Own Recipes

No-cook sauces and dressings are incredibly fun and easy to concoct. Nevertheless, if you are the type of cook who can't function without a recipe or one who follows each recipe to the letter, inventing your own no-cook sauces and dressings may seem like a daunting challenge. Bear in mind, however, that little can go wrong that can't readily be corrected. If you add too much of one ingredient—let's say an acidulant—you can counter the tartness with a little sweetener, a bland liquid, a spoonful of nut butter, some blended tofu or avocado, and so on. There is always a way for the resourceful cook to cleverly salvage a sauce or dressing that's gone awry. Thus, forge ahead with your culinary inventiveness and send those unnecessary worries packing.

The ideal way to season foods when improvising a recipe is to tune in to your culinary intuition. Even if you think yours is missing or dormant, it's there—it may just need a gentle nudge to be awakened. Our senses of smell and taste are closely related. When you sniff your food and then sniff your seasonings with the conscious intent of selecting compatible flavor combinations, you will soon develop an instinctive ability to make appropriate choices. A variety of factors can affect our taste preferences: disposition, age, health, region of the country where we live or were raised, climate, season of the year, and so forth. Some taste combinations that you like today may not be on your list of favorites tomorrow. This is why listening to your "sixth sense" every time you prepare a meal is the only way to be certain you'll be satisfied with the results.

Approach each sauce or dressing as a new and exciting adventure. Evaluate your mood, contemplate the other ingredients of the meal, investigate what needs to be used up in the refrigerator, and explore your cravings. Whatever it takes, let your imagination be stimulated! Select an oil or foundation ingredient and move on from there, gradually incorporating small amounts of a limited number of other ingredients, adding more of them or one or two new ingredients until the taste is just right.

When adding salt, dried herbs, and spices, pinch a small amount between the tips of your thumb and forefinger. Crush the seasoning with your fingers and release a small stream of it as you move your hand in concentric circles or zig-zags over the mixing bowl. Determine the amount of seasoning to use by the amount of sauce or dressing in the bowl. Proceed with prudence. Blend in the seasoning and taste the mixture again after each addition. Season with conscious awareness and you will avoid the pitfall of overseasoning. Let your taste buds guide you, and confer with them regularly. With time and experience, you'll discover a new world of creativity in the kitchen.

Tips for Creating No-Cook Sauces & Dressings

When making no-cook sauces and dressings, always start with the freshest, highest-quality ingredients. This way you'll be assured of robust and distinctive flavors, even when you incorporate a minimal number of components.

Although savory no-cook sauces and dressings often contain similar ingredients, sauces are generally thicker and less sour than dressings and tend to sit on top of food instead of being absorbed by it. Vinaigrettes easily serve double duty as marinades, but even thicker and creamier sauces and dressings can do a respectable job of marinating. Preparation techniques for no-cook sauces and dressings are basically the same. Once a sauce or dressing has been prepared, a resting period of fifteen minutes is recommended, if time permits, to allow flavors to mellow and marry.

Since no-cook sauces and dressings are designed to enhance other foods, they should not be eaten alone. Their flavors should be rich and concentrated so they do not get obscured when combined with other foods.

Some people find the sharp taste of raw onion unpleasant in no-cook sauces and dressings. An easy way to cut the biting edge is to steep chopped onion in equal amounts of vinegar and water for thirty to sixty minutes or longer. The longer the onion steeps, the milder it will become. Drain and rinse the onion, and proceed with the recipe as directed. A less effective but quicker deflaming method is to place chopped onion in a strainer or fine colander and rinse it well under cold water.

If you want to warm a sauce or dressing to create wilted salads or to use over cooked grains, potatoes, pasta, or vegetables, use hot or boiling water instead of room temperature water during the preparation. Your sauce or dressing will be warm and ready to use without any cooking or further heating.

Styles of No-Cook Sauces & Dressings

No-cook sauces and dressings are characterized by their primary ingredients as well as by their viscosity, texture, taste, and energetics. Styles encompass one or more attributes from each of the following categories:

Primary Ingredients:
* avocado
* nuts / seeds
* olives
* vegetables
* beans
* oil
* tofu
* tomatoes / tomato products

Viscosity:
* runny
* thick
* thin
* dense

Texture:
* creamy
* grainy
* smooth
* chunky

Taste:
* sweet
* salty
* bitter
* sour
* pungent
* astringent

Energetics:
* light
* warming
* aromatic
* stimulating
* heavy
* cooling
* soothing

Correcting Flavors

Sometimes recipes need to be tweaked in order to get the flavor just right. Once again, culinary intuition comes into play. Sniff the sauce or dressing, and let the aroma flow through your mind. Put a drop of the sauce or dressing on your tongue, and permit the flavors to spread slowly throughout your mouth. Caress the sauce or dressing between your tongue and palate to determine textural nuances. The process of bringing a recipe to fruition should be a highly focused, sensory experience. What is the recipe telling you? How can you ascertain its energetics? What is it asking for? Mull over the six tastes. Is one or more of them deficient or dominating?

The flavor of overly salty or sour sauces or dressings can be equalized by adding small amounts of mild or bland sweet foods such as blended tofu, blended beans, mashed avocado, and salt-free nut or seed butters. A small amount of torn soft bread or bread crumbs blended with the sauce or dressing can also help to counter too much salt. A pinch of sugar or other sweetener will take the edge off of recipes that are too tart or sour. Conversely, recipes that are too sweet can be balanced with acidulants such as citrus juice or vinegar, or sour foods such as sauerkraut or umeboshi plums.

Every time an ingredient is added, the flavor of a recipe is transformed. Often the process of correcting flavors simultaneously alters the recipe's viscosity, texture, and energetics. Adjust seasonings and incorporate new ingredients methodically and gradually, tasting after every addition. Guard against flavors doing battle for attention. Evaluate again and again. With a little patience and practice, you'll come to sense exactly what each recipe needs. When a recipe works, record what you did. When it doesn't, take note so as not to repeat a blunder. Immerse yourself in the process and, above all, have fun!

Correcting Consistency

Once you begin making the recipes in this book or invent your own no-cook sauces and dressings, you'll discover that some recipes are a little too thick or thin for your particular needs or tastes.

Fine-tuning the consistency of no-cook sauces and dressings can be a bit tricky, especially when you consider that adding ingredients to change the viscosity can upset the delicate balance of flavors. For example, if a recipe contains lemon juice and you add more to make the sauce or dressing thinner, the finished product may very well be too tart. Likewise, if miso is added to a recipe to thicken it, the sauce or dressing may become too salty or acquire an overly strong miso flavor. Most of the recipes in this book were formulated to be on the thicker side because it is somewhat easier to thin a sauce or dressing than it is to thicken it. Also, when you begin with a thicker consistency, you have more flexibility and control over how to use the finished product —either as a sauce or a dressing, if thinned.

Thickening

The following ingredients are useful for thickening a too-thin no-cook sauce or dressing. Bear in mind that these will also alter the flavor, color, texture, and nutritional composition of your recipe in addition to thickening the consistency:

* Blended silken tofu
* Vegan mayonnaise
* Tomato paste or ketchup
* Sweet white miso
* Prepared mustard
* Umeboshi plum paste
* Nut or seed butter
* Nutritional yeast flakes
* Blended beans
* Blended onion

Thinning

The following liquids are useful for thinning a too-thick no-cook sauce or dressing:

➤ Spring or filtered water

➤ Plain nondairy milk (such as soymilk, rice milk, nut milk, oat milk, or others)

➤ Vegetable stock

➤ Vegetable juice (such as carrot juice, tomato juice, or vegetable "cocktail" blend) thinned with an equal amount of water

➤ Vinegars and acidulants thinned with an equal amount of water

➤ Dealcoholized wine

➤ Mild, unsweetened herb tea

Tips for Correcting Consistency

➤ Make modifications slowly and carefully in small, well-calculated increments.

➤ Use ingredients with the same, similar, or complementary flavors as those in the original recipe.

➤ Consider the textural qualities of the original recipe, and incorporate comparably textured additions. For instance, if a sauce or dressing is nut butter-based, add more of the same nut butter to thicken it. If the sauce or dressing is creamy, nondairy milk would be ideal for thinning it.

➤ After adjusting the consistency, taste the sauce or dressing again and correct the seasonings, if necessary.

How to Improvise No-Cook Sauces & Dressings

Select one or more ingredients from each column in the chart on the next page. Blend or whisk them together until they are well combined or form an emulsion. Whisk in water or other liquid, if desired, to achieve a pourable consistency. Taste and adjust the seasonings, if necessary. Use the following proportions as a general guideline: *1 to 3 parts oil or other foundation to 1 part vinegar or acidulant.*

Chart for Improvising Sauces & Dressings

Oils and other Foundations	Vinegars & Acidulants	Salt Seasonings	Herbs, Spices & Seasonings	Sweeteners (optional)
Avocado or olives, mashed or blended ✳ **Oil:** Canola Extra-virgin olive Flaxseed Hazelnut Safflower Walnut Others ✳ **Vegetables,** blended ✳ **Tomato:** Fresh, Paste, Juice Ketchup ✳ **Nuts (blended):** Cashews Pine Nuts Walnuts ✳ **Nut/Seed Butter:** Almond Cashew, Peanut Sesame tahini Others ✳ **Silken tofu,** blended ✳ **Beans,** mashed or blended	**Vinegar:** Apple cider Balsamic Brown rice Fruit Herbal Umeboshi Wine ✳ **Citrus juice:** Grapefruit Lemon Lime Orange ✳ **Umeboshi paste** ✳ **Olive brine** ✳ **Sauerkraut juice**	**Plain or seasoned salt** ✳ **Tamari or shoyu** ✳ **Liquid Aminos** ✳ **Umeboshi:** Paste Vinegar Whole plums ✳ **Miso,** sweet white ✳ **Sauerkraut** and juice ✳ **Olives** and brine	**Herbs:** Basil, Chives Cilantro Dill weed Oregano Parsley Rosemary Tarragon Thyme, Others ✳ **Spices:** Chili powder Curry powder, Cumin, Fennel, Garlic, Ginger, Nutmeg, Paprika, Pepper, Others ✳ **Sesame oil,** dark ✳ **Mustard:** Yellow, Brown Dijon Seasoned Powder ✳ **Nutritional yeast** flakes ✳ **Onion:** Red, White Scallion Shallot ✳ **Capers** ✳ **Horseradish**	**Agave nectar** ✳ **Apple juice** or frozen apple juice concentrate ✳ **Brown rice syrup** ✳ **Granulated maple sugar** or pure maple syrup ✳ **Sugar,** unbleached or raw ✳ **FruitSource** ✳ **Mirin** ✳ **Sorghum syrup**

Worksheet for Improvising No-Cook Sauces & Dressings

Style of Sauce _____

Oil/Foundation Ingredient(s)	**Amount**
_____	_____
_____	_____

Vinegar/Acidulant(s)	**Amount**
_____	_____
_____	_____

Salt Seasoning(s)	**Amount**
_____	_____
_____	_____

Herbs, Spices, Seasoning(s)	**Amount**
_____	_____
_____	_____
_____	_____
_____	_____

Liquid(s)	**Amount**
_____	_____
_____	_____

Sweetener	**Amount**
_____	_____
_____	_____

Notes

_____

_____

_____

_____

_____

_____

Vinaigrette Sauces & Dressings

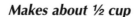

Italian Dressing

Makes about ½ cup

Try this on:
* antipasto
* pasta salad
* three bean
  salad

A delicate blend of Old World herbs and spices add enticing Mediterranean nuances.

¼ cup extra-virgin olive oil

2 tablespoons wine vinegar

1 tablespoon fresh lemon juice

2 teaspoons Dijon mustard

½ teaspoon sugar

½ teaspoon crushed garlic

½ teaspoon *each:* dried basil and oregano

Pinch of salt

Combine all the ingredients in a small bowl, and whisk together until emulsified.

Per tablespoon: Calories 63, Protein 0 g, Fat 7 g, Carbohydrates 0 g

French Vinaigrette

Makes about ⅓ cup

Try this on:
* tossed salad
* marinated
  vegetables
* spinach

A tart and savory dressing that enhances other flavors without overpowering them.

¼ cup extra-virgin olive oil

1 tablespoon wine vinegar

1 tablespoon fresh lemon juice

1 teaspoon Dijon mustard

½ teaspoon crushed garlic

½ teaspoon sugar

¼ teaspoon salt

Dash of pepper

Combine all the ingredients in a small bowl, and whisk together until emulsified.

Per tablespoon: Calories 100, Protein 0 g, Fat 10 g, Carbohydrates 0 g

Yellow Ocher Vinaigrette

Makes about ½ cup

Try this on:
* *millet and black beans*
* *kale and sunflower seeds*
* *quinoa and asparagus*

This irresistible golden vinaigrette brightens the taste of every food it touches. From grains to beans to steamed vegetables, its versatility is boundless.

¼ cup extra-virgin olive oil

2 tablespoons wine vinegar

1 tablespoon fresh lemon juice

2 teaspoons Dijon mustard

2 teaspoons nutritional yeast flakes

1 teaspoon sugar

½ teaspoon crushed garlic

Pinch of salt

Combine all the ingredients in a small bowl, and whisk together until emulsified.

Per tablespoon: Calories 66, Protein 0 g, Fat 7 g, Carbohydrates 1 g

Del Sol Dressing

Makes about 1 cup

Try this on:
* *bibb lettuce*
* *broccoli and raisins*
* *elbow macaroni with fresh basil and tomatoes*

This rich and perky dressing complements every savory dish while contributing the delicious and healthful benefits of nutritional yeast.

¼ cup nutritional yeast flakes

¼ cup extra-virgin olive oil

¼ cup canola oil

¼ cup water

2 tablespoons wine vinegar

½ teaspoon tamari soy sauce

½ teaspoon crushed garlic

Combine all the ingredients in a blender, and process until smooth and creamy.

Per tablespoon: Calories 66, Protein 1 g, Fat 6 g, Carbohydrates 1 g

Parisian Vinaigrette

Makes about ½ cup

Try this on:
* spinach and strawberry salad
* French-cut green beans and slivered almonds
* baby redskin potatoes

A unique and, dare we say, romantic dressing that adds a touch of passion to any dining experience.

¼ cup extra-virgin olive oil
2 tablespoons wine vinegar
1 tablespoon fresh lemon juice
2 teaspoons Dijon mustard
2 teaspoons nutritional yeast flakes
1 teaspoon sugar
½ teaspoon crushed garlic
¼ teaspoon paprika
⅛ teaspoon dry mustard
Pinch of salt

Combine all the ingredients in a small bowl, and whisk together until emulsified.

Per tablespoon: Calories 66, Protein 0 g, Fat 7 g, Carbohydrates 1 g

Herb & Onion Vinaigrette

Makes about ½ cup

Try this on:
* hot or cold potato salad
* marinated vegetables
* romaine and radicchio salad

A piquant marriage of seasonings that is sure to tickle your tongue.

¼ cup extra-virgin olive oil
2 tablespoons wine vinegar
1 tablespoon fresh lemon juice
1 tablespoon chopped onions
1 tablespoon minced fresh parsley
2 teaspoons Dijon mustard
2 teaspoons nutritional yeast flakes
1 teaspoon sugar
¼ teaspoon *each:* dried thyme and oregano
Pinch of salt and pepper

Combine all the ingredients in a blender, and process until smooth.

Per tablespoon: Calories 67, Protein 0 g, Fat 7 g, Carbohydrates 1 g

Chili Lime Dressing

Makes about ½ cup

Modest salads jump to life with this fine blend of Southwestern seasonings. Rice mixtures, bean salads, or any dish with corn will soar to extraordinary heights with just a splash.

⅓ cup extra-virgin olive oil

3 tablespoons fresh lime juice

1 teaspoon ground cumin

½ teaspoon chili powder

½ teaspoon sugar

½ teaspoon crushed garlic

Pinch of salt

Combine all the ingredients in a small bowl, and whisk together until emulsified.

Per tablespoon: Calories 77, Protein 0 g, Fat 8 g, Carbohydrates 0 g

Try this on:
* **corn on the cob**
* **succotash**
* **polenta with broccoli**

Cilantro Lime Vinaigrette

Makes about ⅔ cup

This fresh fusion of flavors enlivens any meal.

3 tablespoons extra-virgin olive oil

3 tablespoons fresh lime juice

3 tablespoons apple cider vinegar

1 tablespoon sweet white miso

1 tablespoon chopped fresh cilantro

1 teaspoon sweetener of your choice

¼ teaspoon crushed garlic

¼ teaspoon salt

Combine all the ingredients in a blender, and process until creamy.

Per tablespoon: Calories 42, Protein 0 g, Fat 4 g, Carbohydrates 1 g

Try this on:
* **quinoa with green peas, grilled onions, and pistachios**
* **corn and black bean salad**
* **avocado and cucumbers**

Lemonade Dressing

Makes about ⅓ cup

Try this on:
* banana, mango, and avocado salad
* Boston lettuce, purple grapes, and pignolia nuts
* pear, raisins, red radishes, and pecans
* couscous with fresh blueberries, dates, and toasted almonds

This deceptively simple dressing will perform feats of wizardry in your kitchen. It's light but packed with a gentle punch, and it's beautifully fat free. Although it's a wonderful all-purpose dressing, it's especially ideal on fruit salads.

¼ cup fresh lemon juice

2 to 4 tablespoons liquid sweetener of your choice

Combine the lemon juice and sweetener in a small bowl, and whisk together until emulsified.

Per tablespoon: Calories 42, Protein 0 g, Fat 0 g, Carbohydrates 11 g

Lemon Vinaigrette

Makes about 1 cup

Try this on:
* grilled tempeh
* shredded carrot, radish, and zucchini salad
* roasted vegetables

When you want something basic but not boring, this is the vinaigrette to rely on. It makes a superb marinade or basting sauce as well as a magnificent dressing.

½ cup fresh lemon juice

½ cup extra-virgin olive oil

2 tablespoons thinly sliced scallions

2 tablespoons minced fresh parsley

½ teaspoon crushed garlic

Salt and pepper

Combine all the ingredients in a small bowl, and whisk together until well blended.

Per tablespoon: Calories 62, Protein 0 g, Fat 7 g, Carbohydrates 1 g

Hot & Spicy Moroccan Vinaigrette

Makes about ¾ cup

Want something a little exotic that will make your dishes pop with flavor? Just keep a pitcher of cold water handy!

½ cup extra-virgin olive oil

¼ cup fresh lemon juice

¼ cup minced fresh parsley

¼ cup chopped fresh cilantro

2 teaspoons ginger juice (see p. 137)

1 teaspoon ground cumin

½ teaspoon crushed garlic

½ teaspoon paprika

¼ teaspoon salt

⅛ to ¼ teaspoon cayenne pepper

⅛ teaspoon pepper

Combine all the ingredients in a blender, and process until creamy.

Per tablespoon: Calories 81, Protein 0 g, Fat 9 g, Carbohydrates 0 g

Try this on:
* **wild rice and diagonally-sliced steamed carrots**
* **thinly sliced cucumbers and walnuts**
* **marinated whole baby mushrooms**

Mirin Dressing

Makes about ¾ cup

Use this delicate dressing to add sprightly tones to any salad or to unify combinations of food.

¼ cup wine vinegar

¼ cup extra-virgin olive oil

¼ cup mirin

⅛ teaspoon salt

Combine all the ingredients in a small bowl, and whisk together until emulsified.

Per tablespoon: Calories 48, Protein 0 g, Fat 4 g, Carbohydrates 0 g

Try this on:
* **lima beans and bulgur**
* **green beans and red bell peppers**
* **steamed vegetables, water chestnuts, and jasmine rice**

Miso Master Dressing

Makes about ¾ cup

Try this on:
* steamed brown rice
* cooked cabbage wedges
* hot pasta spirals with mixed vegetables

Sweet, sour, salty, and rich-tasting—this dressing masters the fine art of flavor balancing.

3 tablespoons sweet white miso
2 tablespoons dark sesame oil
2 tablespoons extra-virgin olive oil
2 tablespoons water
2 tablespoons brown rice vinegar
2 tablespoons brown rice syrup
2 tablespoons chopped onions
1 teaspoon Dijon mustard

Combine all the ingredients in a blender, and process until smooth.

Per tablespoon: Calories 58, Protein 1 g, Fat 5 g, Carbohydrates 4 g

Michael's Red Dressing

Makes about ½ cup

Try this on:
* romaine, arugula, and leaf lettuce salad
* steamed cauliflower
* barley and mushrooms

The perfect sweet and sour dressing to infuse your favorite grains, greens, and vegetables.

¼ cup extra-virgin olive oil
3 tablespoons chopped onions
2 tablespoons apple cider vinegar
1 tablespoon brown rice syrup
¼ teaspoon paprika
⅛ teaspoon dry mustard
⅛ teaspoon salt

Combine all the ingredients in a blender, and process until smooth.

Per tablespoon: Calories 70, Protein 1 g, Fat 5 g, Carbohydrates 4 g

Magical Sesame Dressing

Makes about ½ cup

Tempt your guests, friends, and family with the mesmerizing nuances of this special dressing, and watch the magic begin!

¼ cup brown rice vinegar

¼ cup dark sesame oil

2 teaspoons tamari soy sauce

1 teaspoon sugar

½ teaspoon salt

Combine all the ingredients in a small bowl, and vigorously whisk together until emulsified.

Per tablespoon: Calories 95, Protein 0 g, Fat 7 g, Carbohydrates 9 g

Try this on:
* **brown rice and dried apricots**
* **steamed Brussels sprouts**
* **noodles and thinly sliced mixed vegetables**

Sweet Basil or Cilantro Vinaigrette

Makes about 1 cup

When summertime delivers an abundance of fresh herbs, there's no better choice than this vinaigrette to showcase their special flavor.

½ cup extra-virgin olive oil

½ cup chopped fresh basil or cilantro

3 tablespoons fresh lemon juice

2 tablespoons water

2 teaspoons brown rice syrup

¼ teaspoon crushed garlic

⅛ teaspoon salt

Pinch of pepper

Combine all the ingredients in a blender, and process until well combined.

Per tablespoon: Calories 63, Protein 0 g, Fat 7 g, Carbohydrates 1 g

Try this on:
* **fresh ripe tomatoes**
* **red beans and millet**
* **corn and pimientos**

51

Umeboshi Plum Vinaigrette

Makes about ½ cup

Try this on:
* *brown rice with pepitas (pumpkin seeds)*
* *couscous with chick-peas and parsley*
* *broiled tofu*

Experience the enchantment of umeboshi plum vinegar and dark sesame oil. A melding of captivating tastes awaits you.

3 tablespoons umeboshi plum vinegar
2 tablespoons fresh lemon juice
2 tablespoons canola oil
1 tablespoon dark sesame oil
2 teaspoons sweetener of your choice

*C*ombine all the ingredients in a small bowl, and whisk together until emulsified.

Per tablespoon: Calories 52, Protein 0 g, Fat 5 g, Carbohydrates 1 g

Umeboshi Herb Dressing

Makes about ½ cup

Try this on:
* *marinated lentils*
* *buckwheat kasha and shiitake mushrooms*
* *brown rice and red kidney beans*

This dressing carefully unites Asian and Mediterranean seasonings so it can easily marry with foods from either culture.

¼ cup wine vinegar
3 tablespoons extra-virgin olive oil
1 tablespoon umeboshi plum paste
2 teaspoons chopped shallots or onions
¼ teaspoon *each:* dried thyme and oregano
Dash of pepper

*C*ombine all the ingredients in a blender, and process until smooth.

Per tablespoon: Calories 46, Protein 0 g, Fat 5 g, Carbohydrates 0 g

Olive & Plum Vinaigrette

Makes about ½ cup

This exquisite but uncomplicated sauce is a stalwart kitchen staple and a handy "secret ingredient" whenever you want to add a bit of excitement to food.

¼ cup umeboshi plum vinegar

¼ cup extra-virgin olive oil

Combine the oil and vinegar in a small bowl, and vigorously whisk together until emulsified.

Per tablespoon: Calories 61, Protein 0 g, Fat 7 g, Carbohydrates 0 g

Try this on:
* **green peas and pearl onions**
* **Belgian endive**
* **dandelion greens**

Maple-Mustard Dressing

Makes about ½ cup

Aaaahhh—sweet mustard dressing enhanced with dark sesame oil. Ideal for dipping, saucing, or tossing.

¼ cup dark sesame oil

2 tablespoons brown rice vinegar

1 tablespoon pure maple syrup

1 tablespoon Dijon mustard

Combine all the ingredients in a small bowl, and whisk together until emulsified.

Per tablespoon: Calories 70, Protein 0 g, Fat 7 g, Carbohydrates 2 g

Try this on:
* **steamed cabbage and carrots**
* **broiled tofu strips**
* **Brussels sprouts**

OFFICIALLY NOTED

Sesame Cilantro Vinaigrette

Makes about ⅔ cup

Fresh lime adds tropical energy to this lively multipurpose dressing.

Try this on:
* artichoke hearts
* collard ribbons and pineapple tidbits
* baked rutabaga and onions

¼ cup fresh lime juice

¼ cup dark sesame oil

2 tablespoons canola oil

1 tablespoon apple cider vinegar

½ teaspoon Dijon mustard

½ teaspoon crushed garlic

¼ teaspoon salt

Combine all the ingredients in a small bowl, and whisk together until emulsified.

Per tablespoon: Calories 74, Protein 0 g, Fat 8 g, Carbohydrates 1 g

Sesame-Mustard Sauce

Makes about ¾ cup

Straightforward ingredients create an uncommonly delicious merger as they mingle in this versatile sauce. Serve over warm vegetables or beans or your own special hot combinations.

Try this on:
* broccoli and cauliflower florets
* black beans, corn, and green pepper
* grated red and green cabbage salad

3 tablespoons Dijon mustard

3 tablespoons tamari soy sauce

3 tablespoons pure maple syrup

2 tablespoons dark sesame oil

2 tablespoons water

Combine all the ingredients in a small bowl, and whisk together until emulsified.

Per tablespoon: Calories 41, Protein 0 g, Fat 2 g, Carbohydrates 3 g

Maple-Dijon Vinaigrette

Makes about ⅔ cup

Onions and garlic harmonize gloriously, turning a mix of ordinary ingredients into an extraordinary savory seasoning.

⅓ cup extra-virgin olive oil

2 tablespoons pure maple syrup

2 tablespoons Dijon mustard

2 tablespoons apple cider vinegar

1 tablespoon chopped onions

½ teaspoon crushed garlic

Combine all the ingredients in a blender, and process until creamy.

Per tablespoon: Calories 75, Protein 0 g, Fat 7 g, Carbohydrates 2 g

Try this on:
* *baked yams*
* *corn, basmati rice, and zucchini*
* *baked turnips, rutabagas, and parsnips*

Fennel-Mustard Sauce

Makes about ⅔ cup

Mustard and fennel are heavenly together. Here they invite a pinch of tarragon to lend piquant sophistication. Superb on raw or cooked vegetables, mixed into hot grains or beans, or drizzled on steaming potatoes. Especially delectable on cabbage, cauliflower, and broccoli.

4 tablespoons Dijon mustard

4 tablespoons extra-virgin olive oil

2 tablespoons fresh lemon juice

1 tablespoon sweetener of your choice

1 teaspoon ground fennel

½ teaspoon dried tarragon

Combine all the ingredients in a small bowl, and whisk together vigorously until emulsified.

Per tablespoon: Calories 65, Protein 0 g, Fat 7 g, Carbohydrates 2 g

Try this on:
* *collard ribbons and brown rice*
* *steamed potato chunks*
* *grated carrot, arugula, and leaf lettuce salad*

Tamari Vinaigrette

Makes about ⅓ cup

Try this on:
* *brown rice with grated carrot*
* *broiled mushrooms*
* *mixed baby greens with toasted slivered almonds*

This airy dressing imparts just enough punch to draw out the hidden flavors of shy grains and vegetables.

3 tablespoons extra-virgin olive oil
2 tablespoons brown rice vinegar
1 teaspoon tamari soy sauce
½ teaspoon Dijon mustard
½ teaspoon sugar

Combine all the ingredients in a small bowl, and whisk together until emulsified.

Per tablespoon: Calories 76, Protein 0 g, Fat 8 g, Carbohydrates 0 g

Tamari-Ginger Dipping Sauce

Makes about ½ cup

Try this on:
* *tofu and vegetable kabobs*
* *broiled tempeh squares*
* *roasted asparagus, yellow squash, and cherry tomatoes*

This consummate dipping sauce for grilled tofu and tempeh is not afraid to strut its stuff with vegetables and grains too.

¼ cup tamari soy sauce
2 tablespoons brown rice vinegar
2 tablespoons mirin
½ teaspoon crushed garlic
½ to 1 teaspoon ginger juice (see p. 137)

Combine all the ingredients in a small bowl, and stir together.

Per tablespoon: Calories 12, Protein 1 g, Fat 0 g, Carbohydrates 1 g

Balsamic Dressing

Makes about ½ cup

Sometimes simple is best, and this choice vinaigrette is case in point.

⅓ cup extra-virgin olive oil
2 tablespoons balsamic vinegar
1 teaspoon crushed garlic
½ teaspoon sugar
¼ teaspoon salt

Combine all the ingredients in a small bowl, and whisk together until emulsified.

Per tablespoon: Calories 76, Protein 0 g, Fat 8 g, Carbohydrates 0 g

Try this on:
* elbow macaroni and vegetable salad
* steamed assorted vegetables
* mixed lettuce salad

Asian Balsamic Dressing

Makes about ¾ cup

Fennel and garlic meld with Asian flavors to tastefully bring any dish to life.

¼ cup canola oil
¼ cup balsamic vinegar
¼ cup tamari soy sauce
2 tablespoons mirin
2 teaspoons sugar
½ teaspoon ground fennel seed
¼ teaspoon crushed garlic

Combine all the ingredients in a small bowl, and whisk together until emulsified.

Per tablespoon: Calories 51, Protein 1 g, Fat 4 g, Carbohydrates 2 g

Try this on:
* basmati rice with pignolia nuts
* steamed acorn squash
* braised mustard greens

Tarragon Mustard Vinaigrette

Makes about ⅔ cup

Tarragon and mustard are a traditional combination that brings zing to every corner of your mouth.

⅓ cup extra-virgin olive oil

2 tablespoons wine vinegar

2 tablespoons water

1 tablespoon Dijon mustard

1 teaspoon dried tarragon

½ teaspoon crushed garlic

Try this on:
* red cabbage and millet
* steamed new potatoes
* braised broccoli raab (rapini)

Combine all the ingredients in a small bowl, and whisk together until emulsified.

Per tablespoon: Calories 62, Protein 0 g, Fat 7 g, Carbohydrates 0 g

Herbal Vinaigrette

Makes about ½ cup

An excellent classic dressing with cunning herbal undertones.

⅓ cup extra-virgin olive oil

2 tablespoons balsamic vinegar

1 teaspoon dried basil or dillweed

½ teaspoon crushed garlic

½ teaspoon dry mustard

¼ teaspoon salt

Try this on:
* lettuce and tomato salad
* marinated carrots, celery, and onions
* romaine lettuce and cold steamed green beans

Combine all the ingredients in a small bowl, and whisk together until emulsified.

Per tablespoon: Calories 75, Protein 0 g, Fat 8 g, Carbohydrates 0 g

Roasted Garlic Dressing

Makes about ½ cup

Try this on:
* steamed
  asparagus and
  mushrooms
* baked russet
  potatoes
* baked fennel

Roasted garlic adds surprising depth and dimension, turning any simple dish into a feast.

¼ cup extra-virgin olive oil

3 tablespoons brown rice vinegar

2 tablespoons mirin

2 to 3 cloves roasted garlic, mashed (see p. 136)

⅛ teaspoon cayenne pepper

*C*ombine all the ingredients in a small bowl, and whisk together until emulsified. Alternatively, combine all the ingredients in a blender, and process until smooth.

Per tablespoon: Calories 66, Protein 0 g, Fat 7 g, Carbohydrates 0 g

Caraway Vinaigrette

Makes about ½ cup

Try this on:
* braised
  cabbage
* steamed
  Brussels sprouts
* steamed
  collard greens

A tantalizing vinaigrette that is marvelous on dark leafy greens and all cruciferous vegetables.

¼ cup extra-virgin olive oil

2 tablespoons apple cider vinegar

2 tablespoons apple juice

2 teaspoons sugar

1 teaspoon Dijon mustard

½ teaspoon whole caraway seeds, or ¼ teaspoon ground

Pinch of salt

Several drops of liquid smoke (optional)

*C*ombine all the ingredients in a small bowl, and whisk together until emulsified.

Per tablespoon: Calories 67, Protein 0 g, Fat 7 g, Carbohydrates 2 g

Raspberry Vinaigrette

Makes about ⅔ cup

Try this on:
* steamed kale
* romaine lettuce with mandarin oranges
* raw spinach with toasted walnuts

The quintessential vinaigrette for raw spinach and tender baby greens.

¼ cup extra-virgin olive oil
3 tablespoons fruit-sweetened seedless raspberry jelly
3 tablespoons wine vinegar
1 teaspoon crushed garlic
¼ teaspoon salt
Pinch of pepper

Combine all the ingredients in a blender, and process until smooth.

Per tablespoon: Calories 61, Protein 0 g, Fat 5 g, Carbohydrates 3 g

Raspberry-Lemon Dressing

Makes about ⅓ cup

Try this on:
* apple, celery, raisin, and walnut salad
* steamed green beans with prunes
* romaine lettuce, banana, and toasted pecans

Easy, flavorful, and fat free, this awesome dressing is unsurpassed for perking up fresh fruit salads and fruit and vegetable combinations.

¼ cup frozen raspberry juice concentrate, thawed
2 tablespoons fresh lemon juice

Combine both ingredients in a small bowl, and whisk together until emulsified.

Per tablespoon: Calories 24, Protein 0 g, Fat 0 g, Carbohydrates 6 g

Sesame-Orange Vinaigrette

Makes about ⅓ cup

Grain and vegetable mixtures are especially amenable to the fruity undertones of this soothing vinaigrette.

2 tablespoons frozen orange juice concentrate

2 tablespoons water

2 tablespoons brown rice vinegar

1 tablespoon dark sesame oil

1 teaspoon tamari soy sauce

1 teaspoon sugar

*C*ombine all the ingredients in a small bowl, and whisk together until emulsified.

Per tablespoon: Calories 40, Protein 2 g, Fat 0 g, Carbohydrates 4 g

Try this on:
* **steamed carrots and basmati rice**
* **millet and beets**
* **quinoa, corn, and pistachios**

Sesame Sweet & Sour Dressing

Makes about ½ cup

Any dish or salad can be transformed into a compelling treat with this all-time favorite. Add a few bacon-flavored soy bits, and you'll have created a classic sensation to lure everyone to the table.

¼ cup brown rice vinegar

3 tablespoons dark sesame oil

1 tablespoon sweetener of your choice

Pinch of cayenne pepper

*C*ombine all the ingredients in a small bowl, and whisk together until emulsified.

Per tablespoon: Calories 54, Protein 0 g, Fat 5 g, Carbohydrates 2 g

Try this on:
* **spinach and red (Spanish) onion salad**
* **cucumber and radish wheels**
* **brown rice with scallions and celery**

Sesame Curry Dressing

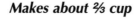

Makes about ⅔ cup

Try this on:
* basmati rice and red beans
* bulgur with shredded carrots
* romaine and red leaf lettuce with bananas

Eastern and Mediterranean tastes collide in a distinctive alliance between two fantastic cuisines.

¼ cup canola oil

¼ cup dark sesame oil

¼ cup fresh lime or lemon juice

1 tablespoon umeboshi plum vinegar

1 teaspoon sweetener of your choice

1 teaspoon curry powder

Pinch of cayenne pepper

*C*ombine all the ingredients in a small bowl, and whisk together until emulsified.

Per tablespoon: Calories 100, Protein 0 g, Fat 10 g, Carbohydrates 1 g

Citrus Vinaigrette

Makes about ½ cup

Try this on:
* baked tempeh and nectarines
* steamed kale
* brown rice and broccoli

An outstanding example of how tart citrus juice can be an excellent replacement for vinegar. This light and refreshing vinaigrette appeals to fruits, vegetables, grains, or beans.

3 tablespoons dark sesame oil

3 tablespoons fresh lemon juice

2 tablespoons frozen orange juice concentrate

1 tablespoon water

2 teaspoons tamari soy sauce

½ teaspoon crushed garlic

½ teaspoon ginger juice (see p. 137)

*C*ombine all the ingredients in a small bowl, and whisk together until emulsified.

Per tablespoon: Calories 54, Protein 0 g, Fat 5 g, Carbohydrates 2 g

Dill Vinaigrette

Makes about ¾ cup

A few innovations turn this basic dressing from humble to sensational!

½ cup apple cider vinegar

¼ cup extra-virgin olive oil

2 teaspoons prepared yellow mustard

1 teaspoon dried dillweed

½ teaspoon crushed garlic

½ teaspoon salt

¼ teaspoon ground fennel seed

¼ teaspoon pepper

Combine all the ingredients in a small bowl, and whisk together until emulsified.

Per tablespoon: Calories 44, Protein 0 g, Fat 4 g, Carbohydrates 1 g

Try this on:
* ✱ *shredded cabbage and carrot slaw*
* ✱ *fettuccine with asparagus tips, red pepper, and water chestnuts*
* ✱ *sliced beets on a bed of watercress and endive*
* ✱ *steamed carrots*

Dill-Dijon Dressing

Makes about ¾ cup

Dill and Dijon are splendid together and make a particularly smashing duo over steamed vegetables or as a dipping sauce for crudités.

⅓ cup brown rice vinegar

⅓ cup dark sesame oil

3 tablespoons pure maple syrup

1½ tablespoons tamari soy sauce

1 tablespoon Dijon mustard

1 teaspoon dried dillweed

Combine all the ingredients in a small bowl, and whisk together until emulsified.

Per tablespoon: Calories 67, Protein 0 g, Fat 5 g, Carbohydrates 3 g

Try this on:
* ✱ *Brussels sprouts*
* ✱ *broiled portobello mushrooms*
* ✱ *avocado and butterhead lettuce*

Nut & Seed Based Sauces & Dressings

Almond-Miso Dressing

Makes about 1¼ cups

Try this on:
* ✳ steamed broccoli and basmati rice
* ✳ tossed lettuce salad with shoestring beets
* ✳ bulgur with chick-peas

This incredible dressing is unparalleled in its ability to unite disparate flavors in hot or cold vegetable combinations.

½ cup crumbled silken tofu

3 tablespoons roasted almond butter

2 tablespoons canola oil

2 tablespoons water

2 tablespoons apple cider vinegar

2 tablespoons sweet white miso

2 tablespoons minced shallots or onions

1 tablespoon sweetener of your choice

1 tablespoon minced fresh parsley

2 teaspoons tamari soy sauce

*C*ombine all the ingredients in a blender, and process until smooth and creamy.

Per tablespoon: Calories 37, Protein 1 g, Fat 3 g, Carbohydrates 2 g

Basil Red Pepper Sauce

Makes about 1 cup

Try this on:
* ✳ grilled tofu
* ✳ raditore pasta
* ✳ steamed mixed vegetables

Blended red bell pepper forms the foundation of a fresh slant on uncooked sauces. Remarkably delicious!

1 red bell pepper, coarsely chopped

2 tablespoons tahini or cashew butter

1 tablespoon Dijon mustard

½ teaspoon dried basil

Pinch of cayenne pepper

Pinch of salt

¼ cup water, more or less as needed

*C*ombine all the ingredients in a blender, and process until smooth and creamy, using just enough water to make a thick but pourable sauce.

Per tablespoon: Calories 13, Protein 0 g, Fat 0 g, Carbohydrates 1 g

Lemon-Nut Dressing

Makes about ½ cup

Try this on:
* **brown rice and vegetable salad**
* **collard greens with pinto beans**
* **baked hubbard squash**

Perfect for steamed vegetables or salads with lots of sturdy ingredients such as grains or beans.

3 tablespoons extra-virgin olive oil
2 tablespoons peanut butter, almond butter, or tahini
2 tablespoons fresh lemon juice
2 tablespoons brown rice vinegar
1 teaspoon sugar
Pinch of salt

*C*ombine all the ingredients in a small bowl, and whisk together until emulsified and smooth.

Per tablespoon: Calories 72, Protein 1 g, Fat 7 g, Carbohydrates 1 g

Mustard-Peanut Sauce

Makes about ⅔ cup

Try this on:
* **baked yams**
* **steamed cabbage wedges**
* **Brussels sprouts**

This is a winner on steamed vegetable and grain combinations and every imaginable kind of legume.

¼ cup smooth peanut butter
¼ cup fresh lemon juice
2 tablespoons prepared yellow mustard
2 tablespoons minced fresh parsley
2 tablespoons water
1 teaspoon sugar
½ teaspoon crushed garlic
Pinch of salt

*C*ombine all the ingredients in a small bowl, and whisk together until emulsified and smooth.

Per tablespoon: Calories46 , Protein 2 g, Fat 3 g, Carbohydrates 2 g

67

Spicy Peanut Sauce

Try this on:
* cold spaghetti with slivered cucumbers
* bok choy and carrots
* brown rice and green peas

Makes about 1 cup

This classic topping for Chinese noodles is also at home on steamed vegetables and grains.

⅓ cup smooth peanut butter

2 tablespoons tamari soy sauce

2 tablespoons brown rice vinegar

1 teaspoon sugar

½ teaspoon crushed garlic

Pinch of cayenne pepper

¼ cup water, more or less as needed

¼ cup thinly sliced scallions, optional

*C*ombine all the ingredients, except the water and scallions, in a small bowl, and whisk together until emulsified and smooth. Gradually whisk in enough water to make a thick but pourable sauce. Stir in the scallions, if using.

Per tablespoon: Calories33 , Protein 2 g, Fat 2 g, Carbohydrates 1 g

Peanuti Salad Dressing

Try this on:
* Chinese cabbage and carrot slaw
* lettuce and cucumber salad
* pasta with green peas and tofu

Makes about 1 cup

Try this irresistible dressing on pasta and vegetables salads.

½ cup peanut butter

1 tablespoon tamari soy sauce

1 tablespoon brown rice vinegar

1 teaspoon dark sesame oil

½ teaspoon crushed garlic

¼ to ½ cup water, more or less as needed

*C*ombine all the ingredients, except the water, in a small bowl, and whisk together until emulsified and smooth. Gradually whisk in enough water to make a thick but pourable sauce.

Per tablespoon: Calories 51, Protein 2 g, Fat 4 g, Carbohydrates 2 g

Warm Peanut-Miso Sauce

Makes about ⅔ cup

Spoon over hot grains and vegetables for a quick and easy entrée.

⅓ cup peanut butter

1 tablespoon sweet white miso

1 teaspoon ginger juice (see page 137)

Pinch of cayenne pepper

½ cup boiling water, more or less as needed

Combine the peanut butter, miso, ginger juice, cayenne pepper, and half the water in a bowl. Mash and beat with a spoon until the mixture forms a smooth paste. Gradually beat in the remaining water, using just enough to form a thick but pourable sauce.

Per tablespoon: Calories 50, Protein 2 g, Fat 4 g, Carbohydrates 2 g

Try this on:
* baked yams
* mashed potatoes
* barley pilaf with mushrooms and scallions

Golden Cashew Cream Sauce

Makes about ½ cup

The whole family will eat their vegetables when they're drizzled with this opulent topping.

⅓ cup cashew butter

1 tablespoon sweet white miso

1½ teaspoons prepared yellow mustard

⅓ cup water, more or less as needed

Combine all the ingredients in a blender, and process until smooth and creamy, using just enough water to make a thick but pourable sauce.

Per tablespoon: Calories 63, Protein 2 g, Fat 5 g, Carbohydrates 3 g

Try this on:
* chopped steamed spinach
* green peas and diced carrots
* wild and brown rice blend with mushrooms

Warm Miso-Almond Gravy

Try this on:
* steamed kale
* baked butternut squash
* noodles and seitan strips

Makes about 1⅓ cups

Greens, grains, and baked winter squash will swoon with delight when topped with this amazing sauce.

6 tablespoons almond butter
4 tablespoons sweet white miso
⅔ cup boiling water, more or less as needed

Combine the almond butter, miso, and half the water in a bowl. Mash and beat with a spoon until the mixture forms a smooth paste. Gradually beat in the remaining water, using just enough to form a thick but pourable gravy.

Per tablespoon: Calories 29, Protein 1 g, Fat 2 g, Carbohydrates 1 g

Cashew "Cheese" Sauce

Try this on:
* wide noodles and green peas
* baked russet potatoes with broccoli
* bow-tie pasta with Swiss chard

Makes about ½ cup

Create instant Alfredo noodles or au gratin dishes with this remarkable dairy-free sauce.

¼ cup raw cashews
1½ tablespoons fresh lemon juice
1½ tablespoons nutritional yeast flakes
2 teaspoons sweet white miso or 1/4 teaspoon salt
½ teaspoon onion powder
Pinch of garlic powder
¼ cup water, more or less as needed

Grind the cashews to a powder in a dry blender. Add the remaining ingredients, using just enough water to make a thick but pourable sauce. Process several minutes until completely smooth.

Per tablespoon: Calories 35, Protein 1 g, Fat 1 g, Carbohydrates 3 g

Cashew Cream

Makes about ¾ cup

Now you can make quick, dairy-free, creamed vegetables, potatoes, and pasta that the whole family will love. Even children will gobble up their vegetables without complaining!

¼ cup cashew butter

Pinch of salt

¼ to ½ cup water, more or less as needed

*P*lace the cashew butter, salt, and water in a blender or food processor fitted with a metal blade, using just enough water to make a thick but smooth sauce. Alternatively, place the cashew butter and salt in a small bowl. Gradually stir in enough water to make a thick but pourable sauce.

Per tablespoon: Calories 31, Protein 1 g, Fat 3 g, Carbohydrates 1 g

Try this on:
* steamed spinach
* lima beans, zucchini, yellow squash, and tomatoes
* broiled portobello mushrooms

Cashew Sour Cream Sauce

Makes about 1 cup

A delectable topping for potatoes, soup, noodles, and more. The perfect sour cream replacement for dairy and soy-sensitive individuals.

½ cup cashew butter

2 tablespoons fresh lemon juice

Pinch of salt

½ cup water, more or less as needed

*C*ombine all the ingredients in a blender or food processor fitted with a metal blade, using just enough water to make a thick but smooth sauce. Alternatively, combine all the ingredients, except the water, together in a small bowl. Gradually stir in enough water to make a thick but pourable sauce.

Per tablespoon: Calories48 , Protein 1 g, Fat 4 g, Carbohydrates 2 g

Try this on:
* baked russet potatoes
* sauerkraut with fresh tomatoes and seitan
* broiled eggplant

Cashew-Sesame Sauce

Makes about ¾ cup

Try this on:
* asparagus tips and quinoa
* roasted mixed vegetables
* spinach and mushroom salad

This luscious sauce marries rich cashew butter and tahini to make a flavorful and satisfying topping for hearty grains, patties, and vegetable loaves.

    2 tablespoons cashew butter
    2 tablespoons tahini
    2 tablespoons fresh lemon juice
    1 tablespoon nutritional yeast flakes
    ½ teaspoon crushed garlic
    ¼ teaspoon salt
    ¼ cup water, more or less as needed

Combine all the ingredients in a blender, and process until smooth and creamy, using just enough water to make a thick but pourable sauce. Alternatively, combine all the ingredients in a small bowl, and whisk together until smooth and well blended, using just enough water to make a thick but pourable sauce.

Per tablespoon: Calories 33, Protein 1 g, Fat 2 g, Carbohydrates 2 g

Miso White Sauce

Makes about ⅔ cup

Try this on:
* polenta with sautéed endive
* udon noodles and steamed vegetables
* spinach fettuccine with chopped fresh tomatoes

An awesome cream sauce for every occasion!

    3 tablespoons tahini
    2 tablespoons sweet white miso
    1 tablespoon fresh lemon juice
    ⅓ cup water, more or less as needed

Combine the tahini, miso, and lemon juice in a small bowl, mixing well to make a thick paste. Gradually stir or whisk in the water, beating well after each addition until smooth, using just enough to achieve the desired consistency.

Per tablespoon: Calories 31, Protein 1 g, Fat 2 g, Carbohydrates 2 g

Tangy Tahini Sauce

Makes about ¾ cup

Try this on:
* artichoke
  hearts
* crudités
* steamed green
  beans

Tart and tangy. You won't believe how creamy and versatile this magnificent sauce is.

¼ cup tahini

2 tablespoons fresh lemon juice

2 tablespoons umeboshi plum vinegar

½ teaspoon crushed garlic

¼ cup water, more or less as needed

Combine all the ingredients in a blender, and process until smooth and creamy, using just enough water to make a thick but pourable sauce. Alternatively, combine all the ingredients in a small bowl, and whisk together until smooth and well blended, using just enough water to make a thick but pourable sauce.

Per tablespoon: Calories 30, Protein 1 g, Fat 2 g, Carbohydrates 2 g

Simple Tahini Dressing

Makes about ¾ cup

Try this on:
* sliced fresh
  tomatoes
* steamed
  asparagus
  spears
* steamed
  Brussels sprouts

All your favorite vegetables will pay homage to this lively sauce.

⅓ cup tahini

1 tablespoon fresh lemon or lime juice

1 tablespoon tamari soy sauce

¼ teaspoon crushed garlic

⅓ cup water, more or less as needed

1 tablespoon minced fresh parsley

Combine the tahini, lemon or lime juice, soy sauce, and garlic in a small bowl, mixing well to make a thick paste. Gradually stir or whisk in the water, beating well after each addition until smooth, using just enough to achieve the desired consistency. Stir in the parsley.

Per tablespoon: Calories 37, Protein 1 g, Fat 2 g, Carbohydrates 2 g

Tahini, Tamari & Onion Dressing

Makes about ⅔ cup

Try this on:
* thinly sliced fresh fennel
* diced cucumber, tomato, and red bell pepper
* bulgur with apricots

Sprightly and spirited, this dressing is right at home wherever it lands.

¼ cup water

2 tablespoons tahini

2 tablespoons minced shallots or onions

1 tablespoon extra-virgin olive oil

1 tablespoon fresh lemon or lime juice

1 tablespoon tamari soy sauce

Combine all the ingredients in a blender, and process until smooth and creamy.

Per tablespoon: Calories 31, Protein 1 g, Fat 2 g, Carbohydrates 1 g

Tantalizing Walnut Sauce

Makes about ¾ cup

Try this on:
* tossed butterhead lettuce salad
* sweet potatoes and kale
* broiled red bell pepper strips

This sauce turns the prosaic into the gourmet.

½ cup walnuts, lightly pan-toasted

1½ tablespoons sweet white miso

1 tablespoon mirin

½ cup water, more or less as needed

Combine the walnuts, miso, and mirin in a blender or food processor fitted with a metal blade, and process until smooth, using just enough water to create a thick but pourable consistency.

Tip: To pan-toast the walnuts, place them in a small, dry skillet over medium-high heat. Stir constantly until they are golden brown and fragrant, about 3 to 4 minutes.

Per tablespoon: Calories 37, Protein 1 g, Fat 3 g, Carbohydrates 1 g

Tahini Poppy Seed Dressing

Makes about 1 cup

A creamy and contemporary sweet and sour dressing.

⅓ cup canola oil

2 tablespoons tahini

2 tablespoons brown rice vinegar

1 tablespoon fresh lemon juice

1 tablespoon minced onions

1 tablespoon sweetener of your choice

2 teaspoons whole celery seeds

¾ teaspoon dry mustard

½ teaspoon crushed garlic

½ teaspoon salt

1 tablespoon poppy seeds

Combine all the ingredients, except the poppy seeds, in a blender, and process until smooth and creamy. Stir in the poppy seeds.

Per tablespoon: Calories 56, Protein 0 g, Fat 5 g, Carbohydrates 2 g

Try this on:
* couscous with artichoke hearts
* baked eggplant steaks
* mashed potatoes

Fennel, Orange & Walnut Sauce

Try this on:
* steamed fennel and green beans
* mushroom and celery salad
* broiled tofu

Makes about 1 cup

Delicately sweet and creamy, this unusual mixture readily adapts to vegetables, fruits, greens, and grains.

½ cup crumbled silken tofu

⅓ cup walnuts, lightly pan-toasted

3 tablespoons brown rice vinegar

2 tablespoons extra-virgin olive oil

1 tablespoon mirin

1 tablespoon frozen orange juice concentrate

1 teaspoon ground fennel seed

¼ teaspoon salt

*C*ombine all the ingredients in a blender, and process until smooth.

Tip: To pan-toast the walnuts, place them in a small, dry skillet over medium-high heat. Stir constantly until they are golden brown and fragrant, about 3 to 4 minutes.

Per tablespoon: Calories 40, Protein 1 g, Fat 3 g, Carbohydrates 1 g

Miso-Ginger Sauce

Makes about 1 cup

Gentle flavors of the East form an unbeatable blend to top vegetables, noodles, grains, or beans.

⅓ cup water

¼ cup sweet white miso

¼ cup tahini

2 tablespoons brown rice vinegar

1 tablespoon mirin

2 teaspoons ginger juice (see p. 137)

½ teaspoon crushed garlic

Pinch of dried tarragon

Combine all the ingredients in a blender or a food processor fitted with a metal blade, and process until smooth.

Per tablespoon: Calories 30, Protein 1 g, Fat 2 g, Carbohydrates 2 g

Try this on:
* *linguine with asparagus tips*
* *lightly steamed cauliflower florets*
* *broiled tempeh*

Creamy Tarragon Dressing

Makes about ½ cup

So quick and easy, this dressing is impeccable on every kind of salad.

¼ cup water

3 tablespoons tahini

2 tablespoons umeboshi plum vinegar

1 teaspoon dried tarragon

Combine all the ingredients in a small bowl, and whisk together until emulsified and smooth.

Per tablespoon: Calories 33, Protein 1 g, Fat 2 g, Carbohydrates 2 g

Try this on:
* *sliced tomatoes on romaine ribbons*
* *orzo pasta with zucchini, artichoke hearts, and white beans*
* *sautéed carrots, mushrooms, and zucchini over bulgur*

Ume Mustard Cream

Try this on:
* soba noodles with blanched snow peas
* avocado and corn salad
* veggie burgers

Makes about ½ cup

A flawless complement to any savory dish.

¼ cup extra-virgin olive oil

2 tablespoons tahini

1 tablespoon umeboshi plum vinegar

1 tablespoon fresh lemon juice

1 tablespoon brown rice vinegar

1 teaspoon Dijon mustard

Combine all the ingredients in a small bowl, and whisk together until emulsified and smooth.

Per tablespoon: Calories 84, Protein 1 g, Fat 8 g, Carbohydrates 1 g

Tahini Tarragon Dressing

Try this on:
* shredded carrot and zucchini salad
* udon noodles and vegetables
* white bean and tomato salad

Makes about 1 cup

An exacting mix of the six tastes that every meal should aim for.

⅓ cup fresh lemon juice

⅓ cup extra-virgin olive oil

2 tablespoons tahini

1 tablespoon crushed garlic

2 teaspoons Dijon mustard

1 teaspoon dried tarragon

½ teaspoon Tabasco sauce

½ teaspoon salt

Pinch of white or black pepper

Combine all the ingredients in a small bowl, and whisk together until emulsified and smooth.

Per tablespoon: Calories 50, Protein 0 g, Fat 5 g, Carbohydrates 1 g

Creamy Orange-Sesame Dressing

Makes about ⅔ cup

A fruity sauce that's fabulous on fruit and lettuce salads as well as simple steamed vegetables.

½ cup orange juice
2 tablespoons tahini
1 tablespoon minced shallots or onions
1 tablespoon balsamic vinegar
2 teaspoons Dijon mustard

*C*ombine all the ingredients in a blender, and process until creamy.

Per tablespoon: Calories 25, Protein 0 g, Fat 5 g, Carbohydrates 1 g

Try this on:
* cold lentil salad
* sweet potato chunks
* sliced bananas, strawberries, and kiwis

Orange-Tahini Dressing

Makes about ½ cup

A dreamy creamy dressing for any raw or cooked salad.

¼ cup orange juice
¼ cup tahini
1 tablespoon fresh lemon juice
1 teaspoon tamari soy sauce
1 teaspoon sweetener of your choice
¼ teaspoon crushed garlic

*C*ombine all the ingredients in a small bowl, and whisk together until emulsified and smooth.

Per tablespoon: Calories 50, Protein 1 g, Fat 2 g, Carbohydrates 4 g

Try this on:
* basmati rice and broccoli
* quinoa and Brussels sprouts
* shredded cabbage and raisins

Herbed Tahini Sauce

Try this on:
* couscous with zucchini, green peas, and tomatoes
* bulgur with chick-peas
* roasted mixed vegetables

Makes about ¾ cup

An exciting new version of a Middle Eastern masterpiece.

¼ cup tahini
¼ cup fresh lemon juice
3 tablespoons water
2 tablespoons minced fresh parsley
1 tablespoon extra-virgin olive oil
1 tablespoon sugar
1 tablespoon minced scallions
1 teaspoon crushed garlic
½ teaspoon lemon zest (optional)
⅛ ground black pepper

Combine all the ingredients in a small bowl, and whisk together until emulsified.

Per tablespoon: Calories 44, Protein 1 g, Fat 3 g, Carbohydrates 3 g

Miso Citrus Sauce

Try this on:
* pink beans with green cabbage and shredded carrots
* corn, bulgur, black beans, and red kidney beans
* basmati rice with coconut shreds

Makes about ¾ cup

Simple, salty, sweet, and savory. An excellent companion to basic grains.

½ cup orange juice
2 tablespoons tahini
2 tablespoons sweet white miso
2 tablespoons minced scallions

Combine all the ingredients in a small bowl, and whisk together until thick and smooth.

Per tablespoon: Calories 23, Protein 1 g, Fat 0 g, Carbohydrates 2 g

Thai Hot & Sour Dressing

Makes about ⅔ cup

Use this fantastic dressing to create quick Pad Thai noodles or a spicy Thai salad. Use crunchy peanut butter for extra texture.

¼ cup fresh lime juice

3 tablespoons peanut butter

2 tablespoons tamari soy sauce

1 tablespoon dark sesame oil

1 tablespoon sugar

1 teaspoon dried basil

½ teaspoon ground ginger

½ teaspoon crushed garlic

½ teaspoon dried spearmint

⅛ teaspoon crushed hot red pepper flakes

*C*ombine all the ingredients in a small bowl, and whisk together until thick and emulsified.

Per tablespoon: Calories 49, Protein 2 g, Fat 3 g, Carbohydrates 3 g

Try this on:
* *baby bok choy*
* *udon noodles with broccoli florets*
* *lettuce and cucumber salad*

Walnut-Miso-Sesame Sauce

Makes about ⅔ cup

This irrepressible topping works for anything you dish up.

⅓ cup walnuts, lightly pan-toasted

3 tablespoons brown rice vinegar

2 tablespoons dark sesame oil

2 tablespoons sweet white miso

2 tablespoons water

2 tablespoons minced shallots or onions

1 tablespoon brown rice syrup

Pinch of cayenne pepper

*C*ombine all the ingredients in a blender, and process until smooth.

Per tablespoon: Calories 61, Protein 1 g, Fat 5 g, Carbohydrates 4 g

Try this on:
* *millet*
* *white beans and steam-wilted escarole*
* *grilled eggplant*

81

Sesame Caesar Dressing

Makes about ⅔ cup

Try this on:
* *torn romaine lettuce with garlic-herb croutons*
* *baked russet potatoes*
* *penne with red kidney beans*

For traditional Caesar salads, nothing could be easier. But don't stop there. This incredible dressing is also a sauce in disguise.

2 tablespoons tahini
2 tablespoons nutritional yeast flakes
2 tablespoons fresh lemon juice
2 tablespoons water
1 tablespoon tamari soy sauce
1 tablespoon Dijon mustard
½ teaspoon crushed garlic

*C*ombine all the ingredients in a small bowl, and whisk together until creamy and smooth. If you prefer a thinner consistency, whisk in additional water.

Per tablespoon: Calories 27, Protein 1 g, Fat 2 g, Carbohydrates 2 g

Sunflower Seed Dressing

Makes about 1 cup

Try this on:
* *spring lettuce mix*
* *sliced ripe tomatoes*
* *brown rice with mushrooms*

Blended sunflower seeds make a rich and novel dressing.

½ cup hulled sunflower seeds
⅔ cup water
3 tablespoons extra-virgin olive oil
3 tablespoons fresh lemon juice
1 tablespoon organic flax oil or additional olive oil
1 tablespoon tamari soy sauce
1 teaspoon *each:* dried tarragon and dillweed
½ teaspoon crushed garlic

*P*lace the sunflower seeds in a dry blender, and grind them into a powder. Add the remaining ingredients, and process several minutes until creamy and smooth.

Per tablespoon: Calories 58, Protein 1 g, Fat 5 g, Carbohydrates 2 g

Sun-Dried Tomato & Spinach Pesto

Makes about 1⅓ cups

Try this on:
* *ziti pasta with great Northern beans*
* *white finger potatoes*
* *whole-grain bagels*

The complexity of flavors in this five-minute sauce belies its ease and elegance.

- 2 cups fresh spinach, stems removed, packed, rinsed, and patted dry
- ½ cup packed fresh basil
- ⅓ cup pignolia nuts
- 2 tablespoons minced oil-packed sun-dried tomatoes, drained
- 2 tablespoons extra-virgin olive oil
- 1½ tablespoons sweet white miso
- ½ teaspoon crushed garlic
- ¼ teaspoon salt
- 1 tablespoon water, more or less, only if needed

*C*ombine all the ingredients in a food processor fitted with a metal blade, adding just enough water to facilitate processing, if needed. Process until fairly smooth.

Per tablespoon: Calories 28, Protein 1 g, Fat 2 g, Carbohydrates 1 g

Walnut Pesto

Makes about ⅔ cup

Try this on:
* *bulgur and white bean salad*
* *spiral pasta with yellow bell peppers*
* *warm Yukon gold potatoes*

A dairy-free pesto for pasta or potatoes. With fresh basil or cilantro, it can't be beat!

1 cup lightly packed fresh basil or cilantro

⅓ cup chopped walnuts

¼ cup extra-virgin olive oil

1½ tablespoons sweet white miso

½ teaspoon crushed garlic

¼ teaspoon salt

1 tablespoon water, more or less as needed

Combine all the ingredients in a food processor fitted with a metal blade, adding just enough water to facilitate processing, if needed. Process until fairly smooth.

Per tablespoon: Calories 77, Protein 1 g, Fat 7 g, Carbohydrates 2 g

Simple Cilantro Sauce

Makes about ½ cup

This sauce celebrates the sensational flavor of cilantro. Spoon it over all your favorite bean, grain, and vegetable combinations.

Try this on:
* *pinto bean burritos*
* *quinoa wraps with corn and fresh tomatoes*
* *basmati rice with red chili beans*

1 cup lightly packed fresh cilantro

2 tablespoons tahini

2 tablespoons fresh lemon juice

½ teaspoon crushed garlic

¼ teaspoon salt

1 to 2 tablespoons water, more or less as needed

Combine all the ingredients in a food processor fitted with a metal blade, adding just enough water to facilitate processing, if needed. Process until fairly smooth.

Per tablespoon: Calories 25, Protein 1 g, Fat 2 g, Carbohydrates 2 g

Red Pepper & Pignolia Sauce

Makes about 1¼ cups

Try this on:
* *whole-grain toast points with tofu and broccoli florets*
* *broiled tempeh steaks*
* *bow tie pasta*

Stupendous! Elegant! Extraordinary! This sauce cannot be beat for its exquisite flavor and incredible versatility. It's sensational on everything from vegetables to bread to pasta and grains.

1 cup roasted red bell peppers (see p. 138), drained

3 tablespoons extra-virgin olive oil

2 tablespoons pignolia nuts, lightly pan-toasted

1 tablespoon balsamic vinegar

1 teaspoon dried basil

1 teaspoon crushed garlic

½ teaspoon salt

Pinch of ground allspice

*C*ombine all the ingredients in a blender or food processor fitted with a metal blade, and process until creamy and smooth.

Tip: To pan-toast the pignolia nuts, place them in a small, dry skillet over medium-high heat. Stir constantly until they are golden brown and fragrant, about 3 to 4 minutes. Remove them immediately from the skillet (otherwise they will stick).

Per tablespoon: Calories 24, Protein 0 g, Fat 2 g, Carbohydrates 1 g

Hot Mustard Plum Sauce

Try this on:
* **broiled tempeh**
* **broiled tofu**
* **soba noodles with carrots and kale**

Makes about ⅔ cup

A fiery dipping sauce loaded with electrifying flavor.

¼ cup sliced scallions
2 tablespoons tahini
2 tablespoons fresh lemon juice
1 tablespoon umeboshi plum paste
½ teaspoon dry mustard powder
Pinch of cayenne pepper
⅓ cup water, more or less as needed

*C*ombine all the ingredients in a blender or food processor fitted with a metal blade, adding just enough water to make a thick but pourable sauce. Process until fairly smooth, but not so much that the contrast is lost between the green scallion and the sauce. Allow the sauce to rest at least 15 minutes before serving so the mustard powder can fully develop its "heat."

Per tablespoon: Calories 29, Protein 1 g, Fat 2 g, Carbohydrates 3 g

I Can't Believe It's Not Cheese Sauce

Makes about 1½ cups

Startle and amaze with this magical but deceptively simple dairy-free "cheese" sauce. Try all the variations for even more taste surprises.

¾ cup water

6 tablespoons tahini

2 tablespoons nutritional yeast flakes

2 tablespoons fresh lemon juice

2 tablespoons chopped onions

2 tablespoons sweet white miso

¼ to ½ teaspoon salt

*P*lace all the ingredients in a blender, and process until creamy and smooth.

For a lower fat version, *reduce the tahini to 2 tablespoons and add ¼ cup silken tofu.*

For a smokey flavor, *add a few drops of liquid hickory smoke.*

For an orange-colored sauce, *reduce the water to ½ cup and add ¼ cup drained pimiento pieces or roasted red bell peppers (see p. 138).*

Per tablespoon: Calories 26, Protein 1 g, Fat 2 g, Carbohydrates 2 g

Try this on:
* elbow macaroni and lima beans
* whole-grain toast points with sliced tomatoes
* Yukon gold potatoes and collard greens

Tomato, Bean & Vegetable Based Sauces & Dressings

Herbed Tomato Sauce

Makes about ¾ cup

Try this on:
* rigatoni and
  green peas
* bulgur and
  chick-peas
* baked whole
  mushrooms

Is it possible to have rich tomato flavor in an uncooked sauce? You bet! Skip slaving over the stove for hours, and serve this lightning-fast alternative instead. Use it wherever tomato sauce is called for—on pasta, polenta, grains, or potatoes.

¼ cup tomato paste

¼ cup extra-virgin olive oil

¼ cup red wine vinegar or balsamic vinegar

1 teaspoon dried basil

½ teaspoon dried oregano

½ teaspoon crushed garlic

¼ teaspoon pepper

2 tablespoons water, more or less as needed

*C*ombine all the ingredients in a small bowl, and whisk together until blended and smooth, using just enough water to achieve a thick but pourable consistency.

Per tablespoon: Calories 45, Protein 0 g, Fat 4 g, Carbohydrates 1 g

Tomato Con Queso Sauce

Makes about 1 cup

Try this on:
* warm corn
  chips
* open-face
  broccoli and
  mushroom
  sandwiches
* vegetable pizza

A speedy and delicious topping for baked potatoes, nacho-style corn chips, or vegetables. Gloriously spicy and cheezy.

1 cup cooked white beans (such as great Northern beans, baby limas, cannellini, navy beans), rinsed and drained

½ cup tomato salsa

3 tablespoons nutritional yeast flakes

2 to 3 tablespoons tahini

2 tablespoons fresh lemon juice

½ teaspoon prepared yellow mustard

¼ teaspoon salt

*C*ombine all the ingredients in a blender, and process until very smooth.

Per tablespoon: Calories 37, Protein 2 g, Fat 0 g, Carbohydrates 5 g

Salsa Fresca

Makes about 1 cup

Nothing beats homemade salsa made with red ripe tomatoes. Cilantro and lime juice add authentic flavors to this zesty relish and topping.

4 roma plum tomatoes, cored, seeded, and chopped

¼ cup chopped red or white onions

¼ cup chopped fresh cilantro

2 tablespoons fresh lime juice or lemon juice

Several drops of Tabasco sauce

Pinch of salt

*C*ombine all the ingredients in a small bowl, and stir together until well combined.

Tip: To seed a tomato, cut the tomato in half crosswise, and gently scoop out the seeds.

Per tablespoon: Calories 8, Protein 0 g, Fat 0 g, Carbohydrates 2 g

Try this on:
* black bean tacos
* cold penne pasta
* green beans with green bell peppers

Rio Grandé Sauce & Marinade

Makes about 1 cup

Add gusto to any dish with this deeply flavored sauce.

1 cup tomato salsa

3 tablespoons nutritional yeast flakes

1 to 2 tablespoons extra-virgin olive oil

1 tablespoon chili powder

½ teaspoon salt

*C*ombine all the ingredients in a small mixing bowl, and whisk together until blended.

Per tablespoon: Calories 21, Protein 1 g, Fat 1 g, Carbohydrates 2 g

Try this on:
* roasted white potatoes, basted with sauce during cooking
* marinated grilled tofu
* marinated baked tempeh

Fresh Tomato & Onion Sauce

Try this on:
* fusilli pasta with white beans and braised endive
* white basmati rice with chickpeas
* grilled polenta

Makes about 1 cup

There is no better way to use up ripe summer tomatoes and fresh basil than with this delightful sauce. It's perfect over pasta, rice, or polenta, but if you have a good Italian bread on hand, dipping may be just the ticket. Add a little olive oil for extra richness, if you like, or serve it as is for fat-free indulgence.

1 large ripe tomato or 4 roma plum tomatoes, cored, seeded and chopped
¼ cup chopped red or white onions
¼ cup chopped fresh basil, or 1½ teaspoons dried basil
1 tablespoon red wine vinegar or balsamic vinegar
Pinch of salt

*C*ombine all the ingredients in a small mixing bowl, and stir together until well combined.

Tip: For a richer sauce, add 2 to 3 tablespoons extra-virgin olive oil.

Per tablespoon: Calories 4, Protein 0 g, Fat 0 g, Carbohydrates 1 g

Sweet Red Pepper Dressing

Try this on:
* broiled eggplant steaks
* grilled tempeh
* sliced baked potatoes

Makes about 1 cup

A colorful and savory addition that elevates the presentation of any food.

1 red bell pepper, coarsely chopped
¼ cup extra-virgin olive oil
2 tablespoons sweet white miso
1 teaspoon sugar
½ teaspoon dried basil

*C*ombine all the ingredients in a blender, and process several minutes until very smooth.

Per tablespoon: Calories 35, Protein 0 g, Fat 2 g, Carbohydrates 1 g

French Tomato Dressing

Makes about 1 cup

Nothing artificial here—this French dressing is the real thing. Made with fresh ingredients and savory seasonings, you'll relish it on far more than salads.

1 small tomato, peeled, seeded, and minced
¼ cup extra-virgin olive oil
3 tablespoons wine vinegar
1 tablespoon fresh lemon juice
1 tablespoon minced fresh parsley
2 teaspoons Dijon mustard
2 teaspoons sugar
1 teaspoon dried basil
¼ teaspoon crushed garlic
Pinch of salt

Combine all the ingredients in a small bowl, and whisk together until blended.

Tip: To peel a tomato, first use a sharp knife to cut a small cross on the bottom of the tomato. Turn the tomato over and cut out the core. Immerse in a pot of boiling water until the skin starts to curl, about 15 to 20 seconds. Remove from the pot using a slotted spoon, and transfer to a bowl of cold water. Let rest until cool. Remove from the water and peel off the skin using your fingers—the skin should peel away easily.

Per tablespoon: Calories 35, Protein 0 g, Fat 3 g, Carbohydrates 0 g

Try this on:
* *elbow macaroni and asparagus*
* *broiled zucchini boats filled with white beans*
* *sliced carrot, celery, and black bean salad*
* *hot or cold green lentils*

No-Cook Barbecue Sauce

Try this on:
* grilled seitan
* butter beans
* broiled zucchini and yellow squash

Makes about 1¼ cups

For tangy barbecue flavor in a jiffy, this recipe is sure to satisfy. Use it to baste grilled veggie burgers, tofu, or tempeh, douse beans, or spice up rice. You'll find endless uses for this truly amazing sauce.

⅓ cup tomato paste

¼ cup tamari soy sauce

¼ cup apple cider vinegar

¼ cup pure maple syrup

2 tablespoons extra-virgin olive oil

1 teaspoon dry mustard

1 teaspoon crushed garlic

¼ teaspoon pepper

Several drops of Tabasco sauce

*C*ombine all the ingredients in a small bowl, and whisk together until blended.

Per tablespoon: Calories 29, Protein 0 g, Fat 1 g, Carbohydrates 3 g

Carrot-Dill Sauce

Try this on:
* steamed cauliflower florets
* lima beans
* brown rice with cut green beans

Makes about 1¼ cups

Fresh raw carrots and a careful blend of complementary seasonings meld into a delectable and unusual sauce that's wonderful over basmati or jasmine rice or any delicate grain or vegetable.

1 cup chopped carrots

½ cup water

2 tablespoons extra-virgin olive oil

1 tablespoon Dijon mustard

1 tablespoon sweet white miso

1 teaspoon dried dillweed

*C*ombine all the ingredients in a blender, and process several minutes until very smooth.

Per tablespoon: Calories 18, Protein 0 g, Fat 1 g, Carbohydrates 1 g

Tomato Ginger Dressing

Makes about 1 cup

Fresh vegetables are blended with the exotic flavors of miso, ginger, and basil to create a colorful and aromatic dressing.

¼ cup chopped carrots
¼ cup chopped onions
¼ cup canola oil
¼ cup apple cider vinegar
2 tablespoons sweet white miso
1 tablespoon tomato paste
1 tablespoon fresh lemon juice
2 teaspoons ginger juice (see p. 137)
1½ teaspoons sugar
½ teaspoon dried basil
Pinch of cayenne pepper

Combine all the ingredients in a blender, and process several minutes until very smooth.

Per tablespoon: Calories 39, Protein 0 g, Fat 3 g, Carbohydrates 1 g

Try this on:
* *broiled mushrooms and asparagus tips*
* *shredded Chinese cabbage*
* *udon noodles*

Garbanzo & Carrot Sauce

Makes about 1 cup

A zippy and vibrant topping.

½ cup cooked garbanzo beans, rinsed and drained
¼ cup chopped raw or cooked carrots
2 tablespoons minced fresh parsley
2 tablespoons chopped onions
1 tablespoon tahini
1 tablespoon umeboshi plum vinegar
¼ cup water, more or less as needed

Combine all the ingredients in a blender, using just enough water to achieve a thick but pourable consistency. Process until smooth and creamy.

Per tablespoon: Calories 15, Protein 1 g, Fat 0 g, Carbohydrates 2 g

Try this on:
* *fettucine*
* *quinoa-stuffed cabbage rolls*
* *brown rice and bulgur pilaf*

Avocado Dressing

Makes about 1 cup

Sumptuous avocado is the feature attraction in this luxurious topping for salads, vegetables, and grains.

    1 ripe Haas avocado (the kind with bumpy skin)
    2 tablespoons chopped shallots or onions
    2 tablespoons extra-virgin olive oil
    2 tablespoons fresh lemon juice or wine vinegar
    ¼ teaspoon salt
    Pinch of pepper
    2 tablespoons water, more or less as needed

Cut the avocado in half lengthwise, twist to separate the halves, discard the pit, and scoop out the flesh with a spoon. Combine the avocado with the remaining ingredients in a food processor or blender, using just enough water to achieve a thick but pourable consistency. Process until smooth. Best if used immediately.

Per tablespoon: Calories 35, Protein 0 g, Fat 3 g, Carbohydrates 1 g

Avocado Salsa Sauce

Makes about 1 cup

Nothing is easier or more enticing than this beguiling delicacy. Use as a relish, dip, or sauce for beans, burgers, or grains.

1 ripe Haas avocado (the kind with bumpy skin)
½ cup tomato salsa

*C*ut the avocado in half lengthwise, twist to separate the halves, discard the pit, and scoop out the flesh with a spoon. Combine the avocado and salsa in a blender or food processor fitted with a metal blade. Process until just blended for a slightly chunky consistency, or longer for a smoother texture. Best if used immediately.*

Per tablespoon: Calories 22, Protein 0 g, Fat 1 g, Carbohydrates 1 g

Try this on:
* mixed vegetable wraps
* mixed bean tacos
* quinoa with corn and red kidney beans

Herb & Vegetable Vinaigrette

Makes about 1 cup

This incomparable combination of fresh vegetables and herbs will turn your concept of vinaigrettes completely upside down.

⅓ cup extra-virgin olive oil
¼ cup minced fresh parsley
¼ cup chopped green or red bell peppers
¼ cup minced or shredded carrot
2 tablespoons brown rice vinegar
2 tablespoons fresh lemon juice
½ teaspoon crushed garlic
¼ teaspoon *each*: dried basil, oregano, and tarragon
¼ teaspoon salt

*C*ombine all the ingredients in a blender, and process until very smooth.*

Per tablespoon: Calories 40, Protein 0 g, Fat 4 g, Carbohydrates 1 g

Try this on:
* assorted lettuces with radicchio and hearts of palm
* radiotore pasta
* asparagus spears and artichoke hearts

Sweet 'n Smoky Vinaigrette

Makes about 1 cup

A unique blend of contrasting flavors in an awesome dressing.

Try this on:
* veggie "meatball" subs
* raw spinach and mushroom salad
* quinoa with corn and green beans
* black-eyed peas and kale

¼ cup ketchup
¼ cup extra-virgin olive oil
¼ cup orange juice
¼ cup brown rice vinegar
2 tablespoons sugar
½ teaspoon crushed garlic
¼ teaspoon salt
¼ teaspoon pepper
Several drops of liquid hickory smoke

Combine all the ingredients in a blender, and process several minutes until smooth and well blended. Alternatively, combine all the ingredients in a small mixing bowl, and vigorously whisk together until emulsified and smooth.

Per tablespoon: Calories 41, Protein 0 g, Fat 2 g, Carbohydrates 3 g

Pink Bean Sauce

Makes about 1 cup

A rich and creamy sauce for grains or pasta, or poured over broccoli or toast points.

½ cup cooked pinto beans, rinsed and drained
  (reserve cooking liquid)
2 tablespoons almond butter
2 tablespoons umeboshi plum vinegar
2 teaspoons crushed garlic
½ cup bean cooking liquid or water, more or less
  as needed

Combine all the ingredients in a blender, using just enough bean cooking liquid or water to achieve a thick but pourable consistency. Process until smooth and creamy.

Per tablespoon: Calories 18, Protein 1 g, Fat 0 g, Carbohydrates 2 g

Try this on:
* *udon noodles with diagonally sliced carrots and mustard greens*
* *chapati and mixed vegetable roll-ups*
* *bulgur and asparagus pilaf*

Tangy White Bean Sauce

Makes about 1 cup

White beans impart a natural creaminess and make the ideal background for a dairy-free no-cook topping.

1 cup cooked white beans (such as great Northern beans,
  baby limas, cannellini, navy beans), rinsed and drained
1 tablespoon fresh lemon juice
1 tablespoon extra-virgin olive oil
1 teaspoon Dijon mustard
1 teaspoon dried tarragon
½ teaspoon crushed garlic
¼ teaspoon salt
Ground white or black pepper
2 tablespoons water, more or less as needed

Combine all the ingredients in a blender, using just enough water to achieve a thick but pourable consistency. Process until smooth and creamy.

Per tablespoon: Calories 21, Protein 1 g, Fat 1 g, Carbohydrates 2 g

Try this on:
* *millet pilaf with carrots, mushrooms, and peas*
* *baked butternut squash*
* *steamed baby Brussels sprouts*

99

Skordalia Sauce

Makes about 1 cup

Try this on:
* *baked potatoes and broccoli*
* *asparagus spears on toast points*
* *linguine and mushrooms*

A rich but not overwhelming sauce that won't overpower other foods. It's outstanding on all cruciferous vegetables as well as potatoes and pasta.

> 1 cup cooked white beans (such as great Northern beans, baby limas, cannellini, navy beans), rinsed and drained
> ¼ cup chopped walnuts
> 1 tablespoon extra-virgin olive oil
> 1 tablespoon fresh lemon juice
> ½ teaspoon crushed garlic
> ¼ teaspoon salt
> 3 to 5 tablespoons water, more or less as needed

Combine all the ingredients in a blender or food processor fitted with a metal blade, using just enough water to achieve a thick but pourable consistency. Process until smooth and creamy.

Per tablespoon: Calories 33, Protein 1 g, Fat 2 g, Carbohydrates 3 g

Hummus Sauce

Makes about 1 cup

Try this on:
* *steamed cabbage wedges*
* *bulgur and rice pilaf*
* *dipping sauce for crudités*

Perfect as a dipping sauce for pita triangles and carrots sticks, it also is fantastic over vegetables and grains.

> 1 cup cooked garbanzo beans, rinsed and drained
> 1 tablespoon extra-virgin olive oil
> 1 tablespoon fresh lemon juice
> 1 teaspoon umeboshi plum vinegar
> ½ teaspoon crushed garlic
> ¼ cup water, more or less as needed

Combine all the ingredients in a blender or food processor fitted with a metal blade, using just enough water to achieve a thick but pourable consistency. Process until smooth and creamy.

Per tablespoon: Calories 24, Protein 1 g, Fat 1 g, Carbohydrates 3 g

Gee Whiz Sauce

Makes about 1½ cups

Imagine a healthful version of the familiar orange cheese sauce from the supermarket. This is it!!! Rich, smooth, and dairy-free! Perfect for pasta, potatoes, or broccoli. Stir a few spoonfuls into soup to add luscious cheezy undertones.

Try this on:
* elbow macaroni and peas
* broccoli spears
* baked russet potatoes

1 cup cooked white beans, rinsed and drained

⅓ cup nondairy milk or water

¼ cup drained pimiento pieces

3 tablespoons nutritional yeast flakes

2 to 3 tablespoons tahini

1½ tablespoons fresh lemon juice

1 tablespoon chopped onions

½ teaspoon prepared yellow mustard

¼ teaspoon salt

Several drops of Tabasco sauce (optional)

*C*ombine all the ingredients in a blender, and process until very smooth and creamy. Add more milk or water, if necessary, to facilitate processing and achieve a thick but pourable sauce.

> **Tip:** Use great Northern beans, baby limas, cannellini, navy, or other white beans of your choice.

Per tablespoon: Calories 27, Protein 1 g, Fat 0 g, Carbohydrates 3 g

Chili Bean Sauce

Makes about 1 cup

Try this on:
* mixed grain and vegetable tacos
* baked corn chips for dipping
* toasted whole-grain bread cubes

Chili lovers will appreciate the simplicity of this no-cook version. It's always a winner over bulgur, rice, millet, quinoa, or hearty whole-grain bread.

1 cup cooked red beans, rinsed and drained

2 tablespoons chopped onions

2 teaspoons fresh lemon juice

2 teaspoons tamari soy sauce

½ teaspoon chili powder

½ teaspoon dried basil

¼ teaspoon ground cumin

Pinch of cayenne pepper

3 to 4 tablespoons water, more or less as needed

Combine all the ingredients in a blender or food processor fitted with a metal blade, using just enough water to achieve a thick but pourable consistency. Process until smooth.

Tip: Use pinto beans, red kidney beans, red chili beans, or other red beans of your choice.

Per tablespoon: Calories 16, Protein 1 g, Fat 0 g, Carbohydrates 3 g

Black Bean Sauce

Makes about 1 cup

Lustrous beans whirl with exotic spices in a fusion of flavors.

1 cup cooked black beans, rinsed and drained
2 tablespoons tahini
2 teaspoons tamari soy sauce
2 teaspoons balsamic vinegar
½ teaspoon crushed garlic
¼ teaspoon ground cumin
¼ teaspoon ground ginger
Pinch of cayenne pepper
3 to 4 tablespoons water, more or less as needed

Combine all the ingredients in a blender or food processor fitted with a metal blade, using just enough water to achieve a thick but pourable consistency. Process until smooth and creamy.

Per tablespoon: Calories 25, Protein 1 g, Fat 0 g, Carbohydrates 3 g

Try this on:
* *stewed winter vegetables*
* *pita bread triangles for dipping*
* *brown rice pilaf with red pepper ribbons and pignolia nuts*

Spicy Red Bean Sauce

Makes about 1 cup

This lively mixture makes a ravishing complement to grains.

1 cup cooked pinto beans, rinsed and drained
2 to 4 tablespoons thinly sliced scallions
2 tablespoons tahini
1 tablespoon red wine vinegar
2 teaspoons tamari soy sauce
¼ to ½ teaspoon Tabasco sauce
¼ teaspoon ground cumin
3 to 4 tablespoons water, more or less as needed

Combine all the ingredients in a blender or food processor fitted with a metal blade, using just enough water to achieve a thick but pourable consistency. Process until smooth.

Per tablespoon: Calories 26, Protein 1 g, Fat 0 g, Carbohydrates 3 g

Try this on:
* *cornbread*
* *mixed grain pilaf*
* *cauliflower florets on toast points*

103

Creamy Tofu Sauces
& Dressings

Classic Ranch Dressing

Makes about ¾ cup

A perennial favorite!

Try this on:
* tossed salad
* veggie burgers
* steamed spinach

¾ cup crumbled silken tofu
2 tablespoons extra-virgin olive oil
1 tablespoon umeboshi plum vinegar
1 tablespoon fresh lemon juice
1 tablespoon water
½ teaspoon dried tarragon
¼ teaspoon crushed garlic
¼ teaspoon dried dillweed
Pinch of dry mustard

Combine all the ingredients in a blender or food processor, and process until smooth and creamy.

Per tablespoon: Calories 32, Protein 1 g, Fat 3 g, Carbohydrates 1 g

Peppercorn Ranch Dressing

Makes about 1 cup

Pungent, peppery, creamy, and grand. Use as a coleslaw dressing, standard salad dressing, or to top baked potatoes.

Try this on:
* open-face mushroom, onion, and seitan sandwiches
* green and red cabbage slaw
* cucumber, bulgur, and radishes in a pita

¾ cup crumbled silken tofu
2 tablespoons extra-virgin olive oil
2 tablespoons fresh lemon juice
2 tablespoons water
1 tablespoon chopped shallots or onions
1 teaspoon dried tarragon
½ teaspoon dried dillweed
¼ to ½ teaspoon coarsely ground pepper
½ teaspoon crushed garlic
½ teaspoon salt

Combine all the ingredients in a blender, and process until smooth and creamy.

Per tablespoon: Calories 24, Protein 1 g, Fat 3 g, Carbohydrates 1 g

Cucumber-Parsley Dressing

Makes about 1 cup

Refreshing and delightful.

½ cup crumbled silken tofu

¼ cup chopped, peeled, and seeded cucumber

¼ cup sliced scallions

¼ cup minced fresh parsley

3 tablespoons fresh lemon juice

2 tablespoons extra-virgin olive oil

½ teaspoon crushed garlic

½ teaspoon salt

⅛ teaspoon pepper

Combine all the ingredients in a blender, and process until very smooth and creamy.

Tip: An English cucumber has a thinner skin than a standard garden cucumber and is virtually seedless.

Per tablespoon: Calories 17, Protein 0 g, Fat 1 g, Carbohydrates 1 g

Try this on:
* *cold brown rice salad*
* *pasta salad*
* *broccoli floret and white bean salad*

Cucumber-Dill Dressing

Makes about 1 cup

Cucumber and dill form a beautiful union in this recipe.

1 cup chopped, peeled, and seeded cucumber

½ cup crumbled silken tofu

2 tablespoons extra-virgin olive oil

2 tablespoons fresh lemon juice

2 tablespoons sweet white miso

1 small scallion, sliced

1 tablespoon chopped fresh dillweed, or 1 teaspoon dried dillweed

Pinch of salt

Combine all the ingredients in a blender, and process until very smooth and creamy.

Per tablespoon: Calories 27, Protein 1 g, Fat 1 g, Carbohydrates 1 g

Try this on:
* *cold couscous with chilled steamed and raw vegetables*
* *tofu stuffed ravioli*
* *brown rice and red beans*

107

Herbs de Provence Dressing

Try this on:
* broiled
  eggplant steaks
* small shell
  pasta
* cold corn and
  lima bean salad

Makes about ⅔ cup

An impressive herbal mélange.

½ cup crumbled silken tofu

2 tablespoons extra-virgin olive oil

2 tablespoons fresh lemon juice

1 tablespoon chopped shallots or onions

1 tablespoon nutritional yeast flakes (optional)

¼ teaspoon pepper

¼ teaspoon *each:* dried thyme, sage, rosemary,
  and ground fennel

¼ teaspoon salt

1 tablespoon water, or more as needed

*C*ombine all the ingredients in a blender or food processor fitted with a metal blade, using just enough water to
achieve a thick but pourable consistency. Process until very
smooth and creamy.

Tip: Allow the dressing to stand for 15 to 20 minutes
  before serving or chill it in the refrigerator to permit the
  flavors of the herbs to blend.

Per tablespoon: Calories 34, Protein 1 g, Fat 3 g, Carbohydrates 1 g

Creamy Herb Dressing

Makes about ⅔ cup

A popular year-round dressing. Use fresh herbs when in season or dry herbs if fresh are unavailable.

¾ cup crumbled silken tofu

2 tablespoons extra-virgin olive oil

2 tablespoons wine vinegar

2 tablespoons fresh dillweed, or 2 teaspoons dried dillweed

1 tablespoon fresh tarragon, or 1 teaspoon dried tarragon

Pinch of salt

Combine all the ingredients in a blender, and process until smooth and creamy.

Per tablespoon: Calories 38, Protein 2 g, Fat 3 g, Carbohydrates 1 g

Try this on:
* sliced tomatoes on a bed of butterhead lettuce
* cucumber and watercress sandwiches
* baked russet potatoes

Herb & Onion Dressing

Makes about 1 cup

This sprightly combination waltzes gracefully with other assertive foods. Makes an excellent partnership with ripe tomatoes, bold salad vegetables, or hearty cooked greens.

½ cup crumbled silken tofu

⅓ cup minced fresh parsley

¼ cup extra-virgin olive oil

2 to 3 tablespoons chopped onions

2 tablespoons apple cider vinegar

1 teaspoon prepared yellow mustard

¾ teaspoon dried oregano

6 fresh basil leaves, or ½ teaspoon dried basil

Pinch of pepper

Combine all the ingredients in a blender, and process until smooth and creamy.

Per tablespoon: Calories 37, Protein 1 g, Fat 3 g, Carbohydrates 0 g

Try this on:
* sliced tomato and cucumber salad
* bulgur with chopped steamed mustard greens
* sliced beets on a bed of romaine lettuce

Herb & Miso Dressing

Makes about 1 cup

Try this on:
* *baked jewel sweet potatoes*
* *spaghetti with hijiki*
* *steamed white potatoes with dulse*

Miso lends a touch of salty tang as it mingles adroitly with pungent herbs and spices.

¾ cup crumbled silken tofu
2 tablespoons extra-virgin olive oil
2 tablespoons sweet white miso
2 tablespoons wine vinegar
2 tablespoons chopped onions
½ teaspoon *each:* dried basil and tarragon
½ teaspoon sugar
¼ teaspoon crushed garlic
¼ teaspoon prepared yellow mustard
⅛ teaspoon ground coriander
Pinch of salt
2 tablespoons water, or more as needed

Combine all the ingredients in a blender, and process until smooth and creamy, using just enough water for a thick but pourable consistency.

Per tablespoon: Calories 28, Protein 1 g, Fat 2 g, Carbohydrates 1 g

Creamy Pesto Sauce

Makes about 1 cup

Try this on:
* *linguine with broccoli florets*
* *Italian bread with sliced tomatoes*
* *steamed Yukon gold potatoes*

The perfect pasta companion!

¾ cup crumbled silken tofu
1 cup lightly packed fresh basil or cilantro
¼ cup pignolia nuts (pine nuts) or walnuts
2 tablespoons sweet white miso
2 tablespoons extra-virgin olive oil
½ teaspoon crushed garlic
¼ teaspoon salt

Combine all the ingredients in a blender, and process until fairly smooth.

Per tablespoon: Calories 40, Protein 2 g, Fat 3 g, Carbohydrates 1 g

Green Olive & Nori Dressing

Makes about 1 cup

A salad of crisp romaine hearts and garlicky croutons will beg to be topped with this impossibly good combination.

Try this on:
* crudités
* baked tortilla chips
* steamed broccoli florets

¾ cup crumbled silken tofu

5 pitted green olives

¼ cup water

1 tablespoon green nori flakes

1 tablespoon fresh lemon juice

2 teaspoons olive brine

1½ teaspoons nutritional yeast flakes

1½ teaspoons Dijon mustard

½ teaspoon crushed garlic

¼ teaspoon *each:* salt and pepper

2 tablespoons extra-virgin olive oil

*C*ombine all the ingredients, except the olive oil, in a blender or food processor fitted with a metal blade, and process until completely smooth. With the blender or processor running, slowly drizzle in the olive oil.

Per tablespoon: Calories 74, Protein 7 g, Fat 2 g, Carbohydrates 7 g

111

Caper & Dill Sauce

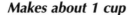

Try this on:
* steamed cauliflower florets
* broiled tempeh cutlets
* wilted cabbage

Makes about 1 cup

A rousing good topping!

¾ cup crumbled silken tofu
2 tablespoons extra-virgin olive oil
2 tablespoons fresh lemon juice
2 tablespoons fresh dillweed, or 2 teaspoons dried dillweed
1 tablespoon drained capers
1 tablespoon water
½ teaspoon crushed garlic
Pinch of salt

Combine all the ingredients in a blender or food processor fitted with a metal blade, and process until smooth and creamy.

Per tablespoon: Calories 24, Protein 1 g, Fat 2 g, Carbohydrates 1 g

Creamy Dill Sauce

Try this on:
* asparagus tips and artichoke hearts
* boiled Jerusalem artichokes and green beans
* roasted red peppers and summer squash

Makes about 1 cup

Burgers, loaves, and casseroles will find bliss when bathed in this enchanting sauce.

1 cup crumbled silken tofu
2 tablespoons extra-virgin olive oil
2 tablespoons sweet white miso
3 tablespoons fresh dillweed, or 1 tablespoon dried dillweed
¼ cup sliced scallions
Pinch of cayenne pepper

Combine all the ingredients in a blender or food processor fitted with a metal blade, and process until smooth and creamy.

Per tablespoon: Calories 29, Protein 2 g, Fat 2 g, Carbohydrates 1 g

Heavenly Horseradish Sauce

Makes about 1 cup

Finally—a cream sauce that bites back!

½ cup crumbled silken tofu

2 tablespoons extra-virgin olive oil

2 tablespoons mirin

2 tablespoons brown rice vinegar

2 tablespoons prepared white horseradish (not creamed)

¼ cup sliced scallions

2 tablespoons minced fresh parsley

2 teaspoons prepared yellow mustard

½ teaspoon crushed garlic

Pinch of salt and pepper

*C*ombine all the ingredients in a blender or food proces-sor fitted with a metal blade, and process until smooth and creamy.

Per tablespoon: Calories 25, Protein 1 g, Fat 1 g, Carbohydrates 0 g

Try this on:
* grilled veggie burgers
* Brussels sprouts and chestnuts
* tofu croquettes

Celery Seed Dressing

Makes about ¾ cup

Mild and different.

¾ cup crumbled silken tofu

2 tablespoons extra-virgin olive oil

2 tablespoons fresh lemon juice

¼ cup sliced scallions

½ teaspoon whole celery seeds

*C*ombine all the ingredients in a blender, and process until creamy.

Per tablespoon: Calories 32, Protein1 g, Fat 3 g, Carbohydrates 1 g

Try this on:
* steamed red potatoes
* cold navy beans and sliced celery
* steamed and crumbled tempeh salad with diced carrot, red onion, and pickle relish

113

Apricot-Celery Seed Dressing

Try this on:
* salad of mango and purple grapes on romaine leaves
* grilled Vidalia onion salad
* salad of chick-peas, orange segments, and slivered almonds on mesclun mix

Makes about 1 cup

Sweet and savory. Great for fruit or vegetable salads.

¾ cup crumbled silken tofu
2 tablespoons canola oil
¼ cup fruit-sweetened apricot jam
2 tablespoons brown rice vinegar
1 tablespoon chopped onions
½ teaspoon whole celery seeds
Dash *each*: pepper and dry mustard

Combine all the ingredients in a blender, and process until creamy.

Per tablespoon: Calories 27, Protein 1 g, Fat 2 g, Carbohydrates 3 g

Curried Apricot Dressing

Try this on:
* quinoa and roasted vegetable salad
* basmati rice with coconut, currants, chopped apples, and cashews
* couscous with chick-peas and shredded spinach

Makes about ¾ cup

Curry harmonizes with sweet or savory tastes, so be daring with this dressing—don't hold back now!

¾ cup crumbled silken tofu
2 tablespoons fruit-sweetened apricot jam
2 tablespoons apple cider vinegar
1 tablespoon canola oil
1 tablespoon chopped onions
½ teaspoon curry powder

Combine all the ingredients in a blender, and process until creamy.

Per tablespoon: Calories 29, Protein 1 g, Fat 2 g, Carbohydrates 2 g

Sweet & Sassy Curry Sauce

Makes about ¾ cup

Citrus and curry make awesome companions. Equally fantastic on salad greens with grapes or pears with peanuts as it is with beans and kale.

¾ cup crumbled silken tofu

2 tablespoons canola oil

2 tablespoons sweetener of your choice

2 tablespoons frozen orange juice concentrate

1 tablespoon fresh lemon juice

½ to 1 teaspoon curry powder

Pinch of salt and pepper

Combine all the ingredients in a blender or food processor fitted with a metal blade, and process until creamy.

Per tablespoon: Calories 44, Protein 1 g, Fat 2 g, Carbohydrates 3 g

Try this on:
* *brown rice, black beans, and orange slices*
* *sliced Bosc or Bartlett pears, raspberries, and toasted walnuts on radicchio*
* *steamed kale, red onion rings, strawberries, blueberries, and orange slices*

Sweet & Mild Mustard Sauce

Makes about ⅔ cup

Dark leafy greens were made for this sauce. Brussels sprouts, broccoli, cauliflower, and cabbage are wild for it too!

½ cup crumbled silken tofu

¼ cup canola oil

2 tablespoons pure maple syrup

2 tablespoons water

1 tablespoon Dijon mustard

¼ teaspoon dry mustard

Pinch *each:* salt and pepper

½ teaspoon poppy seeds

Combine all the ingredients, except the poppy seeds, in a blender or food processor fitted with a metal blade, and process until creamy. Stir in the poppy seeds.

Per tablespoon: Calories 68, Protein 1 g, Fat 5 g, Carbohydrates 2 g

Try this on:
* *medley of steamed turnips, beets, and red onions*
* *melon ball salad with cantaloupe, honeydew, and watermelon*
* *slaw of shredded green cabbage, shredded carrot, and dried cherries*

Creamy Italian-Style Dressing

Try this on:

* ✳ **warm rotini with collard green ribbons and thinly sliced button mushrooms**
* ✳ **shredded leaf lettuce, halved cherry tomatoes, shredded carrot, great Northern beans**
* ✳ **thinly sliced fennel and zucchini half-moons**

Makes about 1 cup

An impeccable alternative to vinaigrette-style Italian dressing. Adds body and boldness with subtle Italian seasonings.

¾ cup crumbled silken tofu

2 tablespoons extra-virgin olive oil

2 tablespoons water

1 tablespoon wine vinegar

1 tablespoon fresh lemon juice

2 teaspoons Dijon mustard

2 teaspoons minced fresh parsley

½ teaspoon crushed garlic, or 1 teaspoon chopped shallots or onions

½ teaspoon *each:* dried basil and oregano

¼ teaspoon pepper

Pinch of salt

*C*ombine all the ingredients in a blender, and process until creamy.

Per tablespoon: Calories 25, Protein 1 g, Fat 2 g, Carbohydrates 0 g

Ravigote

Makes about 1 cup

Try this on:
* *steamed new potatoes*
* *broiled tempeh cutlets*
* *cooked wheat berries with pinto beans*

A tart, sour, and savory blend that will make your burgers, loaves, and cutlets sing!

1 cup crumbled silken tofu
2 tablespoons extra-virgin olive oil
1 tablespoon chopped dill pickle or drained dill pickle relish
1 tablespoon minced fresh parsley
1 small scallion, sliced
2 teaspoons tamari soy sauce
2 teaspoons fresh lemon juice
2 teaspoons wine vinegar
1 teaspoon Dijon mustard
1 teaspoon drained capers
1 teaspoon dried tarragon
¼ teaspoon salt

*C*ombine all the ingredients in a blender, and process until creamy.

Per tablespoon: Calories 28, Protein 1 g, Fat 2 g, Carbohydrates 1 g

Maple-Poppy Seed Dressing

Makes about ⅔ cup

A creamy and mild dressing that is perfect for any fruit salad.

Try this on:
* shredded red cabbage and carrot slaw
* chopped celery, carrots, and apricots
* diced Bartlett pears, crisp red apples, dates, and figs

¾ cup silken tofu, crumbled
2 tablespoons canola oil
1 tablespoon poppy seeds
1 tablespoon pure maple syrup
1 tablespoon fresh lemon juice
Pinch of salt
1 tablespoon water, more or less as needed

Combine all the ingredients in a blender, using just enough water to achieve a thick but pourable consistency. Process until creamy.

Per tablespoon: Calories 43, Protein 2 g, Fat 3 g, Carbohydrates 2 g

Thousand Island Dressing

Makes about ¾ cup

A classic for tossed salad, this dressing is also at home on baked potatoes, steamed vegetables, and beans. In addition, it makes a stupendous sandwich spread in place of mayonnaise.

Try this on:
* veggie burgers
* seitan and sauerkraut sandwiches
* grilled tofu steaks with lettuce on whole-grain buns

½ cup crumbled silken tofu
2 tablespoons ketchup
1½ tablespoons lightly drained pickle relish
1 tablespoon extra-virgin olive oil
1 tablespoon fresh lemon juice
1 tablespoon chopped onions, or ½ teaspoon onion powder
⅛ teaspoon salt

Combine all the ingredients in a blender or food processor fitted with a metal blade, and process until creamy.

Per tablespoon: Calories 23, Protein 1 g, Fat 1 g, Carbohydrates 2 g

Creamy Coleslaw Dressing

Makes about ¾ cup

Shred crunchy vegetables of any shade—carrots, red cabbage, green cabbage, peppers, turnips, radishes, and more—spoon on the dressing, and you've got coleslaw! Add a few toasted nuts or seeds, if you like. Go ahead—bend the rules!

¾ cup crumbled silken tofu
2 tablespoons canola oil
2 tablespoons fresh lemon juice
2 tablespoons frozen apple juice concentrate
1 tablespoon whole celery seeds, caraway seeds, or
  poppy seeds
Pinch of salt

Combine all the ingredients in a blender, and process until creamy.

Per tablespoon: Calories 37, Protein 1 g, Fat 2 g, Carbohydrates 2 g

Try this on:
* matchstick parsnips boiled until tender-crisp
* sliced celery and cold kidney beans with toasted walnuts
* steamed winter squash cubes and black beans

Creamy Tarragon-Dijon Dressing

Makes about 1 cup

A zippy dressing for all occasions.

¾ cup crumbled silken tofu
3 tablespoons extra-virgin olive oil
2 tablespoons wine vinegar
1 tablespoon fresh lemon juice
2 teaspoons Dijon mustard
1 teaspoon dried tarragon
⅛ teaspoon pepper
Pinch of salt

Combine all the ingredients in a blender or food processor fitted with a metal blade, and process until creamy.

Per tablespoon: Calories 32, Protein 1 g, Fat 3 g, Carbohydrates 1 g

Try this on:
* udon noodles with lima beans
* brown basmati rice with cashews and currants
* couscous with lentils

119

Lemon-Caper Dressing

Try this on:
* pan-fried tempeh
* baked spaghetti squash
* arborio rice with chick-peas and Swiss chard

Makes about ¾ cup

Zap your taste buds with this inspired, creamy concoction.

½ cup crumbled silken tofu
¼ cup fresh lemon juice
2 tablespoons extra-virgin olive oil
2 teaspoons drained capers
1 teaspoon sugar
½ teaspoon Dijon mustard
½ teaspoon crushed garlic
¼ teaspoon dried thyme
⅛ teaspoon pepper
Pinch of salt
1 tablespoon minced red bell pepper (optional)

Combine all the ingredients, except the red bell pepper, in a blender or food processor fitted with a metal blade, and process until creamy and smooth. Stir in the red bell pepper, if using.

Per tablespoon: Calories 30, Protein 1 g, Fat 3 g, Carbohydrates 1 g

Lemon-Basil Dressing

Try this on:
* brown rice with corn and roasted green bell peppers
* cold cubed butternut squash and spaghetti
* succotash

Makes about ¾ cup

Lightly sweet and sharp, fresh basil is the secret ingredient.

½ cup crumbled silken tofu
2 tablespoons fresh lemon juice
2 tablespoons extra-virgin olive oil
1 tablespoon chopped onions
1 tablespoon fruit-sweetened apricot jam
Pinch *each*: salt and pepper
6 large fresh basil leaves, sliced into strips

Combine all the ingredients, except the basil leaves, in a blender or food processor fitted with a metal blade, and process until creamy. Stir in the basil leaves.

Per tablespoon: Calories 32, Protein 1 g, Fat 3 g, Carbohydrates 1 g

Lemon-Scallion Dressing

Makes about 1 cup

A toothsome match for baked tempeh or tofu.

½ cup crumbled silken tofu
¼ cup sliced scallions
3 to 4 tablespoons fresh lemon juice
2 tablespoons extra-virgin olive oil
2 tablespoons sweet white miso
1 tablespoon chopped fresh basil, or ½ teaspoon dried basil
1 to 2 tablespoon water, more or less as needed

Combine all the ingredients in a blender or food processor fitted with a metal blade, using just enough water to achieve a thick but pourable consistency. Process until very smooth and creamy.

Per tablespoon: Calories 25, Protein 1 g, Fat 1 g, Carbohydrates 1 g

Try this on:
* rice and avocado-stuffed nori rolls
* steamed cubed potatoes and lentils
* millet with black soybeans

Lemon-Sesame Cream

Makes about 1 cup

This spread and dip imparts richness and flavor to any meal.

½ cup crumbled silken tofu
¼ cup tahini
2 tablespoons fresh lemon juice
2 tablespoons apple cider vinegar
2 tablespoons sweetener of your choice
2 tablespoons water
1 tablespoon sweet white miso
¼ teaspoon crushed garlic
Pinch of salt

Combine all the ingredients in a blender or food processor fitted with a metal blade, and process until creamy.

Per tablespoon: Calories 30, Protein 1 g, Fat 2 g, Carbohydrates 2 g

Try this on:
* udon noodles with steamed kabocha squash and nori flakes
* white beans with parsley
* whole-wheat linguine with sun-dried tomatoes

Creamy Tomato Dressing

Makes about ¾ cup

Try this on:
* seitan and sauerkraut on rye bread
* broiled tempeh
* baked potato wedges for dipping

A simple Russian-style dressing for salads or sandwiches. Try it with seitan and sauerkraut on rye, with a pickle on the side.

½ cup crumbled silken tofu
2 tablespoons extra-virgin olive oil
2 tablespoons tomato paste
2 tablespoons wine vinegar
1 tablespoon fresh lemon juice
1 tablespoon water
½ teaspoon crushed garlic
½ teaspoon sugar
⅛ teaspoon pepper
Pinch of salt

Combine all the ingredients in a blender or food processor fitted with a metal blade, and process until creamy.

Per tablespoon: Calories 65, Protein 2 g, Fat 3 g, Carbohydrates 2 g

Tunisian Cream Sauce

Makes about 1 cup

Try this on:
* steamed redskin potatoes
* cabbage and noodles
* medley of steamed cauliflower and broccoli florets

This toothsome sauce was inspired by the dazzling flavors of Tunis. You can make it as hot and spicy as you like.

1 cup crumbled silken tofu
2 tablespoons fresh lemon juice
2 tablespoons extra-virgin olive oil
½ teaspoon ground (or 1 teaspoon whole) caraway seed
½ teaspoon ground coriander
½ teaspoon salt
½ teaspoon crushed garlic
⅛ teaspoon cayenne pepper

Combine all the ingredients in a blender or food processor fitted with a metal blade, and process until creamy.

Per tablespoon: Calories 27, Protein 1 g, Fat 2 g, Carbohydrates 1 g

Peanut-Chili Whip

Makes about ¾ cup

A flavorful topping or dip for raw or cooked vegetables, bread, chips, or crackers. Don't forget steamed potatoes and green beans too!

½ cup crumbled silken tofu

2 tablespoons fresh lime or lemon juice

2 tablespoons balsamic vinegar

2 tablespoons smooth peanut butter

1 teaspoon dark sesame oil

½ teaspoon crushed garlic

½ teaspoon chili powder

Pinch of salt

Combine all the ingredients in a blender or food processor fitted with a metal blade, and process until creamy.

Per tablespoon: Calories 28, Protein 2 g, Fat 2 g, Carbohydrates 1 g

Try this on:
* *green beans with water chestnuts*
* *steamed butternut squash*
* *baked yams*

Tarator Cream

Makes about 1 cup

An ultra-creamy version of the traditional Mediterranean topping. Great on chilled artichoke hearts, warm steamed vegetables, or as a dip for pita bread.

¾ cup crumbled silken tofu

¼ cup fresh lemon juice

2 tablespoons tahini

½ teaspoon crushed garlic

¼ teaspoon dried oregano

Pinch *each:* salt, pepper, and paprika

Combine all the ingredients in a blender or food processor fitted with a metal blade, and process until creamy.

Per tablespoon: Calories 20, Protein 1 g, Fat 1 g, Carbohydrates 1 g

Try this on:
* *chilled artichoke hearts*
* *cauliflower florets garnished with fresh cilantro*
* *toasted pita triangles for dipping*

Roasted Garlic Aïoli

Try this on:
* steamed mixed vegetables
* oven-fried potato nuggets
* linguine with asparagus tips

Makes about 1½ cups

Just a touch of this French-inspired sauce will make pasta, potatoes, and vegetables irrepressible.

1 large head of garlic, roasted (see p. ??)
1½ cups crumbled silken tofu
3 tablespoons extra-virgin olive oil
1 tablespoon nutritional yeast flakes
1 tablespoon fresh lemon juice
½ teaspoon Dijon mustard
½ teaspoon salt

*R*oast the garlic according to the directions on p. ??. Allow the garlic to cool. Slice off the top and squeeze the roasted cloves from the skin into the bowl of a food processor fitted with a metal blade or in a blender. Add the remaining ingredients, and process several minutes until very smooth and creamy.

Per tablespoon: Calories 29, Protein 1 g, Fat 2 g, Carbohydrates 1 g

Orange Aïoli

Try this on:
* mandarin orange salad with steamed tempeh
* salad of navel oranges, ripe tomatoes, and red onion on bibb lettuce
* cannellini beans, pitted ripe olives, and watercress in butterhead lettuce cups

Makes about 1 cup

A unique topping for noodles, rice, and steamed vegetable combinations. Sweet, savory, and garlicky.

¾ cup crumbled silken tofu
3 tablespoons frozen orange juice concentrate
2 tablespoons extra-virgin olive oil
1½ teaspoons prepared yellow mustard
1½ teaspoons fresh lemon juice
½ teaspoon crushed garlic
Pinch of salt

*C*ombine all the ingredients in a blender, and process until smooth.

Per tablespoon: Calories 29, Protein 1 g, Fat 2 g, Carbohydrates 2 g

Quick Curry Dressing

Makes about ⅔ cup

Thick and flavorful, this dressing is great as a dip or topping.

½ cup crumbled silken tofu
2 tablespoons brown rice vinegar
1 tablespoon extra-virgin olive oil
1 tablespoon fresh lemon juice
1 teaspoon curry powder
½ teaspoon sugar
¼ teaspoon *each*: paprika and chili powder
Pinch of salt

Combine all the ingredients in a food processor fitted with a metal blade, and process until very smooth and creamy.

Per tablespoon: Calories 22, Protein 1 g, Fat 2 g, Carbohydrates 1 g

Try this on:
* *roasted asparagus spears on a bed of chopped romaine lettuce*
* *papaya and watercress salad*
* *salad of corn, French-cut green beans, and julienned carrots, zucchini, yellow summer squash, and red bell peppers*

Roasted Red Pepper Sauce

Makes about 1½ cups

A rich, rosy sauce that will brighten the appearance and taste of any food it touches.

1 cup roasted red bell peppers (see p. ??)
½ cup crumbled silken tofu
2 tablespoons extra-virgin olive oil
2 tablespoons fresh lemon juice
1 tablespoon sweet white miso
¼ teaspoon *each:* pepper, dry mustard, and ground ginger
¼ teaspoon crushed garlic
Pinch of salt

Combine all the ingredients in a blender, and process until smooth.

Per tablespoon: Calories 17, Protein 1 g, Fat 1 g, Carbohydrates 1 g

Try this on:
* *roasted potatoes with broccoli and beets*
* *grilled green bean and eggplant salad*
* *brown and wild rice mixed with peas and toasted slivered almonds*
* *baked spaghetti squash*

Creamy Onion Dressing

Makes about ¾ cup

Try this on:
* roasted red peppers and steamed new potatoes
* steamed Yukon Gold potatoes with minced dill pickles and diced red bell peppers
* brown rice with sliced red radishes, green bell peppers, celery, and parsley

The classic dressing for potatoes—chips, oven fries, steamed, or baked in the jacket.

¾ cup crumbled silken tofu

¼ cup chopped onions

3 tablespoons fresh lemon juice

2 tablespoons extra-virgin olive oil

1 tablespoon minced fresh parsley

½ teaspoon crushed garlic

¼ teaspoon dried dillweed

¼ teaspoon salt

Pinch of pepper

Combine all the ingredients in a blender, and process until smooth.

Per tablespoon: Calories 33, Protein 1 g, Fat 3 g, Carbohydrates 1 g

Creamy Balsamic Dressing

Makes about ⅔ cup

Try this on:
* long-grain brown rice with roasted red bell peppers, pitted oil-cured ripe olives, and scallions
* shell pasta with watercress, cucumber, and red onion
* greens beans with hijiki, matchstick summer squash, and red radishes

The exquisite flavor of balsamic vinegar in a gentle, appetizing dressing.

¾ cup crumbled silken tofu

1 tablespoon extra-virgin olive oil

1 tablespoon balsamic vinegar

2 teaspoons fresh lemon juice

2 teaspoons tamari soy sauce

½ teaspoon crushed garlic

¼ teaspoon pepper

Pinch of salt

Combine all the ingredients in a blender, and process until creamy.

Per tablespoon: Calories 27, Protein 2 g, Fat 2 g, Carbohydrates 1 g

Glorious Green Olive Dip & Dressing

Makes about ¾ cup

Brace yourself—no matter what you serve this striking sauce with, your guests will beg you for the recipe!

¾ cup crumbled silken tofu

¼ cup lightly packed fresh cilantro or basil

3 pitted green olives

1 tablespoon fresh lemon juice

2 teaspoons nutritional yeast flakes

2 teaspoons Dijon mustard

½ teaspoon crushed garlic

¼ teaspoon salt

⅛ teaspoon pepper

2 tablespoons extra-virgin olive oil

*C*ombine all the ingredients, except the olive oil, in blender or a food processor fitted with a metal blade, and process until completely smooth. With the processor running, slowly drizzle in the olive oil.

Per tablespoon: Calories 35, Protein 1 g, Fat 3 g, Carbohydrates 1 g

Try this on:
* *thinly sliced fennel on Boston lettuce*
* *salad of steamed cauliflower, string beans, and wax beans with cherry tomatoes and avocado on red leaf lettuce*
* *spring lettuce mix with avocado, radishes, and navel oranges*

Green Ecstasy Dressing

Makes about 1½ cups

Try this on:
* whole-wheat pasta shells with asparagus and carrots
* shredded daikon radish on Bibb lettuce
* sliced ripe tomatoes on a bed of mesclun mix

Send your taste buds to nirvana with the heavenly flavor of this creamy green sauce.

1 ripe Haas avocado (the kind with bumpy skin)

½ cup crumbled silken tofu

2 tablespoons extra-virgin olive oil

2 tablespoons wine vinegar

2 tablespoons sweet white miso

2 tablespoons chopped shallots or onions

½ teaspoon crushed garlic

2 tablespoons water, more or less as needed

2 tablespoons minced fresh parsley

Cut the avocado in half lengthwise, twist to separate the halves, discard the pit, and scoop out the flesh with a spoon. Combine the avocado and remaining ingredients, except the parsley, in a blender or food processor fitted with a metal blade, using just enough water to achieve a thick but pourable consistency. Process until smooth. Stir or pulse in the parsley. Best if used immediately.

Per tablespoon: Calories 30, Protein 1 g, Fat 1 g, Carbohydrates 2 g

Instant Alfredo Sauce

Makes about 2¼ cups

No one will believe this sauce is low in fat and dairy-free. Toss it with fettuccine and wait for the accolades to begin.

*T*ry this on:
* ✶ steamed redskin potatoes
* ✶ elbow macaroni with grated carrot and yellow summer squash, with parsley garnish
* ✶ basmati rice with kale

½ pound crumbled firm regular tofu, steamed 5 minutes and cooled

3 tablespoons nutritional yeast flakes

2 tablespoons tahini

2 tablespoons fresh lemon juice

1½ tablespoons sweet white miso

1 teaspoon onion powder

¾ teaspoon salt

½ teaspoon paprika

¼ teaspoon *each:* garlic powder and dry mustard

½ to 1 cup water, more or less as needed

*P*lace all the ingredients, except the water, in a food processor fitted with a metal blade, and process until very smooth. Stop the processor occasionally to stir the mixture, and scrape down the sides of the container. Blend in the water, adding a small amount at a time to make a thick but pourable sauce.

Tip: For Warm Alfredo Sauce, do not cool the tofu and use boiling water.

Per tablespoon: Calories 13, Protein 1 g, Fat 0 g, Carbohydrates 1 g

Sour Dressing

Try this on:
* baked russet potatoes
* salad of raspberries, bananas, mango, and pecans
* cold cantaloupe soup

Makes about 1½ cups

A magnificent dairy-free sour cream.

1½ cups crumbled silken tofu
2 tablespoons fresh lemon juice
1 tablespoon white wine vinegar
½ teaspoon salt
⅛ teaspoon ground coriander
2 tablespoons canola oil

Combine all the ingredients, except the oil, in a blender, and process until creamy. With the blender running, drizzle in the oil in a slow steady stream through the cap opening in the blender lid. Chill. Stir before serving.

Per tablespoon: Calories 22, Protein 1 g, Fat 2 g, Carbohydrates 1 g

Tofu Sour Cream

Try this on:
* potato pancakes
* borscht
* noodle kugel

Makes about ¾ cup

Another low-fat twist on the renowned dairy topping.

¾ cup crumbled silken tofu
1 tablespoon extra-virgin olive oil
1 teaspoon fresh lemon juice
1 teaspoon apple cider vinegar
¼ teaspoon sugar
¼ teaspoon salt

Combine all the ingredients in a blender or food processor fitted with a metal blade, and process until creamy. Chill. Stir before serving.

Per tablespoon: Calories 22, Protein 1 g, Fat 2 g, Carbohydrates 1 g

No-Cook Hollandaise

Makes about 1 cup

You will be awed by the beauty and flavor of this majestic sauce. Asparagus tips, of course, but don't forget broccoli, cauliflower, carrots, green beans, and any other favorite vegetables.

1 cup crumbled silken tofu

2 tablespoons extra-virgin olive oil

2 tablespoons water

1 tablespoon fresh lemon juice

1 tablespoon nutritional yeast flakes

1 tablespoon tahini

1 teaspoon prepared yellow mustard

½ teaspoon dried tarragon

1/4 + turmeric

*C*ombine all the ingredients in a blender or food processor fitted with a metal blade, and process until creamy. Chill. Stir before serving.

Per tablespoon: Calories 34, Protein 2 g, Fat 2 g, Carbohydrates 1 g

Try this on:
* asparagus spears
* carrots and green beans
* kasha (roasted buckwheat) pilaf with corn and peas

Umeboshi Mayonnaise

Makes about 1 cup

An utterly stupendous spread.

1 cup crumbled silken tofu

2 tablespoons extra-virgin olive oil

1 tablespoon umeboshi plum vinegar

¼ teaspoon crushed garlic

*C*ombine all the ingredients in a blender or food processor fitted with a metal blade, and process until creamy. Chill. Stir before serving.

Per tablespoon: Calories 26, Protein 1 g, Fat 2 g, Carbohydrates 1 g

Try this on:
* roasted tofu sandwiches
* grain burgers
* crostini (toasted Italian bread)

131

Deli Dressing

Try this on:
* potato salad
* grilled polenta
  with sautéed
  mushrooms
* marinated
  grilled tofu
  layered with
  tomato fans

Makes about 1½ cups

A delightful tofu-based mayonnaise.

1½ cups crumbled silken tofu
3 tablespoons fresh lemon juice
½ teaspoon salt
¼ teaspoon dry mustard
¼ cup canola oil

Combine all the ingredients, except the oil, in a blender, and process until creamy. With the blender running, drizzle in the oil in a slow steady stream through the cap opening in the blender lid. Chill. Stir before serving.

Per tablespoon: Calories 32, Protein 1 g, Fat 2 g, Carbohydrates 1 g

Low-Fat Egg-Free Mayonnaise

Makes about ¾ cup

A fat-reduced spread with full-speed flavor.

¾ cup crumbled silken tofu
1 tablespoon extra-virgin olive oil
1 teaspoon fresh lemon juice
1 teaspoon apple cider vinegar
1 teaspoon sugar
Heaping ¼ teaspoon salt
¼ teaspoon prepared yellow mustard

Try this on:
* tofu-stuffed
  blintzes
* radicchio leaves
  filled with
  pineapple and
  pecans
* fruit kabobs
  (apple chunks,
  orange sections,
  banana slices,
  strawberry
  halves, kiwi
  slices,
  pineapple
  chunks)

Combine all the ingredients in a blender or food processor fitted with a metal blade, and process until creamy. Chill. Stir before serving.

Per tablespoon: Calories 23, Protein 1 g, Fat 2 g, Carbohydrates 1 g

Creamy Potato Salad Dressing

Makes about 1 cup

For a quick and easy potato salad, make this dressing and just add potatoes—in or out of the jacket, red, blue, white, golden, or sweet. Stir in any other ingredients you desire—let your imagination soar! Perfect for macaroni salad too.

¾ cup crumbled silken tofu

¼ cup sliced scallions

2 tablespoons extra-virgin olive oil

2 tablespoons fresh lemon juice

2 tablespoons prepared yellow mustard

2 tablespoons brine from pickles

2 teaspoons sugar

½ teaspoon whole celery seeds

¼ teaspoon pepper

Pinch of salt

Dash of paprika

2 tablespoons minced fresh parsley

*C*ombine all the ingredients, except the parsley, in a *blender or food processor fitted with a metal blade, and process until creamy. Stir in the parsley.*

Per tablespoon: Calories 29, Protein 1 g, Fat 2 g, Carbohydrates 1 g

Try this on:
* *chilled blanched carrots, kale, cabbage, and red onions*
* *sliced bok choy, steamed and chilled, with pecans*
* *tricolor spiral pasta with radicchio*

Special Additions

Roasted Garlic

1 large head of garlic
1 teaspoon extra-virgin olive oil

*U*sing your hands, rub or peel off as much papery skin *from the garlic as can be removed easily while still keeping the head intact. (A thin layer of the papery skin should still remain.) Brush or rub the garlic liberally with the olive oil. Place in a small, shallow baking dish (or on a small, double folded sheet of silver foil with the edges turned up) in the toaster oven (to save energy), and roast it at 325°F until the innermost cloves are soft, about 40 to 60 minutes.*

Tips: Roasted garlic adds a rich, mellow flavor to dressings and sauces without the bite of raw garlic.

* You can use roasted garlic measure for measure to replace raw garlic in all your recipes. If you find you use it often, this recipe can easily be doubled. This way you'll be sure to always have some on hand.

* Roasted garlic will keep for at least two weeks unpeeled and stored in an airtight container in the refrigerator.

Ginger Juice

*S*queezing grated ginger extracts its juice and releases its concentrated flavor. It's the perfect way to incorporate fresh ginger flavor to sauces without adding fibrous strands or small pieces of minced ginger.

The best way to grate ginger is to use a specially designed, inexpensive tool called a "ginger grater," which has tiny teeth designed to gnaw through even the most fibrous root and turn it into a creamy purée. Ginger graters are sold at Asian and natural food stores and cookware shops.

To make ginger juice, cut off an inch or two of fresh gingerroot. Rinse it under water, and pat it dry. (It is not necessary to peel the ginger.) Grate it finely on a ginger grater. Place the grated ginger in the center of a piece of cheesecloth, a clean cotton towel, or a clean cotton napkin that has been spread out over a small bowl. Gather up the sides of the cloth around the ginger, and twist them tightly. The ginger will form a small ball beneath the twisted cloth. Squeeze the ginger firmly and the juice will run into the bowl below.

Tips: Ginger juice will lose its strength and pungency when stored; it is best to squeeze it just before you need to use it.

* Store the fresh gingerroot in the refrigerator wrapped in a clean cotton towel or napkin. It will keep for about two weeks.

Roasted Red Peppers
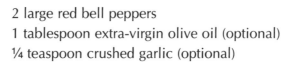
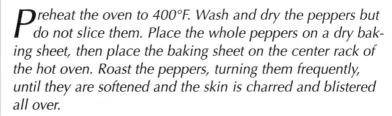

2 large red bell peppers
1 tablespoon extra-virgin olive oil (optional)
¼ teaspoon crushed garlic (optional)

*P*reheat the oven to 400°F. Wash and dry the peppers but do not slice them. Place the whole peppers on a dry baking sheet, then place the baking sheet on the center rack of the hot oven. Roast the peppers, turning them frequently, until they are softened and the skin is charred and blistered all over.

Remove the peppers from the oven, and place them in an empty pot or bowl. Cover the pot with a lid or the bowl with a plate, and allow the peppers to steam for 20 to 25 minutes. Remove the peppers and peel off the loosened skin with your fingers. (Do not rinse the peppers under water as this will wash away much of the flavor.) Remove the stems, seeds, and ribs, and discard them.

Cut the peppers into thick strips, and place them in a clean, small bowl. Sprinkle with olive oil and garlic, if using, and toss gently. Serve warm or thoroughly chilled.

> **Tips:** Choose heavy peppers with thick, meaty flesh. Light, thin peppers will burn before their skin chars.
>
> ✳ Roasted red pepper strips impart a luscious flavor and eye-catching color to sauces and dressings. They are also great as a condiment, garnish, or salad ingredient.
>
> ✳ Jarred roasted red bell peppers are available in most supermarkets and may be substituted equally for home roasted peppers in recipes. They may be served plain or marinated in a little olive oil and garlic, if desired. Drain before using.

Marinated Sun-Dried Tomatoes

1 cup dry-packed sun-dried tomatoes
Extra-virgin olive oil, as needed

Steam the tomatoes until soft, about 5 minutes. Transfer to a jar and pour in enough olive oil to cover the tomatoes completely. Seal the jar and marinate in the refrigerator for at least 2 days before using. Stored in the refrigerator, marinated tomatoes will keep for at least 2 months.

> **Tip:** When chilled, olive oil congeals. Therefore, allow the tomatoes and oil to come to room temperature before using. This will re-liquefy the oil.

Tahini-Miso Foundation Spread & Sauce

This sauce and dressing is exceptionally adaptable. Although it is delicious as is, it can also be enhanced with fresh or dried herbs, minced garlic or onion, fresh ginger juice, or other seasonings of your choice.

1 part sweet white miso
1 part tahini
1 to 2 parts water
Several drops dark sesame oil, to taste

Place all the ingredients in a mixing bowl, and beat together with a wooden spoon or wire whisk until smooth and creamy. Use the smaller amount of water for a spread and the larger amount of water for a sauce.

> **Tip:** This is a great spread for toast or bagels. It is also easily converted to a creamy sauce for grains, pasta, potatoes, beans, or vegetables by simply beating in additional water.

Tamari-Roasted Seeds & Nuts

½ cup raw seeds or nuts
Tamari soy sauce or Bragg Liquid Aminos

*P*lace the seeds or nuts in a skillet over medium-high heat. Toast, stirring almost constantly with a wooden spoon, until the they are evenly light brown, make a slight crackling sound, and emit a nutty aroma. Remove the skillet from the heat. Sprinkle a small amount of tamari soy sauce or Liquid Aminos over the hot seeds or nuts, using just enough to lightly coat them. Quickly toss the seeds or nuts in the hot skillet to dry them, and evenly distribute the soy sauce or Liquid Aminos. Transfer to a shallow bowl or plate, and allow to cool.

Variations: Add a pinch of chili powder, curry powder, ground ginger, or nutritional yeast flakes to the seeds or nuts just before or after adding the tamari soy sauce or Liquid Aminos.

＊ For Ume-Roasted Seeds and Nuts, omit the tamari or Liquid Aminos and instead use a small amount of umeboshi plum vinegar.

Tips: Some good choices for seeds and nuts include sunflower, pumpkin, cashews, almonds, and walnuts.

＊ Tamari-roasted and ume-roasted seeds and nuts make a delightful, savory garnish for grain, bean, and vegetable dishes, and are a nutritious, crunchy addition to salads.

＊ Pumpkin seeds will make a popping sound and puff up when they are toasted.

Index

You can purchase these best-selling vegan cookbooks at your local bookstore or natural foods store, or directly from the publisher:

Book Publishing Company
P.O. Box 99
Summertown, TN 38483
1-800-695-2241
www.bookpubco.com

Please add $3.00 per book
for shipping and handling.

By Joanne Stepaniak

**The Uncheese
Cookbook
$12.95**

**Table for Two
$12.95**

**Ecological Cooking
(with Kathy Hecker)
$10.95**

**Delicious
Food for a
Healthy Heart
$12.95**

**Vegan Vittles
$12.95**

**The Nutritional
Yeast Cookbook
$9.95**